William Bewick, Thomas Landseer

Life and letters of William Bewick

William Bewick, Thomas Landseer

Life and letters of William Bewick

ISBN/EAN: 9783742827265

Manufactured in Europe, USA, Canada, Australia, Japa

Cover: Foto ©Andreas Hilbeck / pixelio.de

Manufactured and distributed by brebook publishing software (www.brebook.com)

William Bewick, Thomas Landseer

Life and letters of William Bewick

LIFE AND LETTERS

OF

WILLIAM BEWICK

(ARTIST).

EDITED BY
THOMAS LANDSEER, A.R.A.

IN TWO VOLUMES.
VOL. II.

LONDON:
HURST AND BLACKETT, PUBLISHERS,
13 GREAT MARLBOROUGH STREET.
1871.

The right of Translation is reserved.

CONTENTS

OF

THE SECOND VOLUME.

CHAPTER I.

LETTER TO MR. CHATFIELD — IMPRESSIONS OF GENOA — WORKS OF ART — OF PAUL VERONESE — COLLECTION IN THE PALAZZO BRIGNOLE — FIRST IMPRESSIONS ON LANDING — HEAD-DRESS OF GENOESE LADIES — GENOESE 'BEAU NASH' — SPEZIA — ITALIAN SERVANT-GIRL — REMINISCENCES OF HOME — THE CAMPAGNA — CROSSING THE TIBER — DISTANT VIEW OF ROME — ST. PETER'S — INN AT TIVOLI — RUINS OF ADRIAN'S VILLA — LETTERS TO HIS SISTER . . . 1–30

CHAPTER II.

MR. BEWICK'S ILLNESS — LANDLADY WITH A GLASS EYE — LADY WESTMORELAND — TABLEAUX VIVANTS — MRS. CHENIE — LIVING IN ROME — SCOTCH AND ENGLISH IN ROME — WILKIE — THE HOLY WEEK — EASTER SUNDAY — MAGNIFICENT PROCESSION — THE CARNIVAL — PRACTICAL JOKING — THE FUN OF CARNIVAL — MASKED BALL . . . 31–55

CHAPTER III.

ERECTION IN THE SISTINE CHAPEL—APPROACH OF SUMMER—OPERA BY A LADY—TWO UNFORTUNATE FRIENDS—FONTANA DELLA DEA EGERIA—CHAPEL OF THE MADONNA—EXCURSION IN THE NEIGHBOURHOOD OF ROME—ALBANO—THE CAFFE AT RICCIA—THE GERMAN ARTIST ON HIS TRAVELS—VILLAGE OF GENTANO—BATHS OF NOCERA—PLEASANT ENTERTAINMENT—A STORM 56–77

CHAPTER IV.

ROME—ENGLISH RESIDENTS IN ROME—EX-QUEEN OF WESTPHALIA—VISIT TO NAPLES—IMPRESSIONS OF THE CITY—NEAPOLITANS FINE DANCERS, BUT REMARKABLY UGLY—DEPRESSING EFFECT OF MOUNT VESUVIUS—ASCENT OF THE MOUNTAIN—POMPEII AND HERCULANEUM—PURCHASE OF ORIGINAL DRAWINGS OF THE OLD MASTERS FOR SIR THOMAS LAWRENCE—SIR THOMAS'S DELIGHT WITH THE 'SIBYL'—FURTHER COMMISSIONS . . . 78–119

CHAPTER V.

RETURN TO ENGLAND—HIS LABOURS WARMLY APPROVED BY SIR THOMAS LAWRENCE—ENCOUNTER WITH HIS OLD FRIEND HAZLITT—INTERVIEW WITH NORTHCOTE—HOUSE IN GEORGE STREET, HANOVER SQUARE—ACCOUNT OF BEWICK'S DRAWINGS IN THE 'ART-UNION'—LETTERS TO TWO FRIENDS—REMINISCENCES OF HIS ARTISTIC EDUCATION—ART-LANGUAGE . . . 120–147

CHAPTER VI.

CONTINUATION OF CORRESPONDENCE WITH MR. DAVISON—A FRIEND OF KEATS THE POET—ADVICE TO HIS FRIEND—MR. SEVERN—PYNE THE ARTIST—PORTRAIT OF MARY BENTON—EXHIBITION OF HIS CARTOONS DESIRED AT NEW YORK—TURNER—REMINISCENCES OF GREAT ARTISTS—LETTERS TO MRS. DAVISON 148–168

CHAPTER VII.

CORRESPONDENCE WITH MR. DAVISON CONTINUED—LEIGH HUNT, KEATS, AND HAYDON—'GROUNDS' OF THE OLD PAINTERS—HAYDON'S AUTOBIOGRAPHY—HIS ABSURD THEORIES—GREEK AND GOTHIC ARCHITECTURE—THE CARTOONS BY NIGHT-LIGHT—EXHIBITION OF ART-TREASURES AT MANCHESTER—EXHIBITION OF FRENCH PICTURES AT NEWCASTLE—LANDSCAPE-PAINTING—A FAVOURITE GREEN—REMINISCENCE OF FLORENCE—THE TURNER GALLERY—MEETING WITH AN OLD FRIEND—RABY CASTLE . . . 169–216

CHAPTER VIII.

CORRESPONDENCE WITH THOMAS H. CROMEK, ESQ.—HOMŒOPATHY—VORACIOUSNESS OF COLLECTORS OF AUTOGRAPHS—HAYDON'S COPY OF REYNOLDS' LECTURES—LIFE AND WORKS OF BLAKE—NOLLEKENS SMITH—ROMAN ARTISTS—SKETCH OF GEORGE THOMPSON—ANATOMICAL STUDIES—PORTRAIT OF T. BEWICK—TERCENTENARY OF SHAKESPEARE—MISS MITFORD—NATHAN ROBSON—PROFESSOR PEPPER—LORD BYRON'S LETTERS—FUSELI . . . 217–253

CHAPTER IX.

CLOSE OF BEWICK'S CAREER—HIS REPUTATION AS AN ARTIST—HIS TASTE FOR LITERATURE—POLITICAL VIEWS—ADVICE TO A YOUNG FRIEND—HIS ARTISTIC ACTIVITY IN THE NORTH OF ENGLAND—OCCUPATION OF HIS DECLINING YEARS—HIS DEATH . . . 254–262

LIFE AND LETTERS

OF

WILLIAM BEWICK.

CHAPTER I.

LETTER TO MR. CHATFIELD—IMPRESSIONS OF GENOA—WORKS OF ART—OF PAUL VERONESE—COLLECTION IN THE PALAZZO BRIGNOLE—FIRST IMPRESSIONS ON LANDING—HEAD-DRESS OF GENOESE LADIES—GENOESE 'BEAU NASH'—SPEZIA—ITALIAN SERVANT-GIRL—REMINISCENCES OF HOME—THE CAMPAGNA—CROSSING THE TIBER—DISTANT VIEW OF ROME—ST. PETER'S—INN AT TIVOLI—RUINS OF ADRIAN'S VILLA—LETTERS TO HIS SISTER.

THE following letter to Mr. Chatfield gives a very minute account of Bewick's temporary sojourn at Genoa, and of the impressions produced upon him by that city.

Rome, September 21st, 1826.

At Genoa, I arrived wearied with a six-weeks' voyage by sea. Here I remained for a week, delighted with the splendour of the palaces that compose the greater portion of this rich city. I was not less pleased, and more excited, by the distant view of the city and its environs from the Gulf of Genoa. Perhaps, it might be owing to its extent and novelty (as seen from 'on board a ship' with a telescope) that it excited the interest I felt; for it is a strong feeling that curiosity perhaps dictates, when a person is transported from his native land, is for the first time boxed-up in a vessel, and sees little all the way but the waves and the sky; the Barbary coast, Gibraltar, and perhaps Cadiz, at a great distance. A strange town, with strange buildings, strange people, and strange noises of bells, must be, and is, very striking to one who has lived as it were—for a month or five weeks on the sea—amphibiously, and seeing nothing but a porpoise, a dolphin, or some ugly monster. Had I come by France, effects would have been gradual, and not so perceptible.

In Genoa there are comparatively few good pictures or works of art. At the Hospital *dei*

Poveri there is a bas-relief of a dead Saviour and Madonna. The head of the former is beautiful, and tranquil in expression, and the hands of the latter equally to be admired for their exquisite form and grace. But the rest is poor and unequal, and cannot certainly have been by this great man. It is of an oval shape, and only contains the two heads and two hands. The head of the Madonna in expression and drawing is dreadful. There are many things here that are said to be by Michael Angelo, that are not only doubtful, but impossible.

Of Paul Veronese there is a large picture, the Anointing Christ's feet, from which there is a print. It is painted (as are all the large pictures of this master) in a bold, large, and grand style. In painting it, the oil seems to have been absorbed quickly, as the touches are dragged very much, and done with full, large brushes,—perhaps these bold, striking lights were painted after the picture was dry. The head of the principal female has its toning taken off, and it looks raw and pinky, though beautiful—more beautiful than most of the heads by this master. There is a weeping expression about the cheeks and eyes that is affecting. Some parts of the picture are vulgar and unmeaning, and some parts quite a study for style. This is in the palace of the Grand Duke, which contains many bad pictures.

In the Palazzo Brignole there are some excellent Vandycks; one, a whole-length, on a grey horse with a broad long tail, is capital for its breadth and simplicity of effect. It is the portrait of the Marquis Antonio Julio Brignole, where the whole picture is made subservient to the head, which is brilliant and Titianesque, and shines out from a darkish, blue-grey sky.

The Prince of Orange, too, is by the same hand, and is very fine.

The portrait of a young Venetian nobleman in a black dress over armour,—a rich gold-handled sword by his side, upon which his left hand rests gracefully, his right taking his hat from a table covered with crimson velvet ornamented with gold. A crimson curtain is behind, with a bit of landscape and twisted column at the right corner. He stands firm, yet graceful, and has the true nobleman look. His frill comes up to his chin and round his throat, like some of Titian's heads, but the whole picture puts you in mind of Velasquez. Indeed, the general character of their minds and genius does not seem to have been dissimilar.

'The Jews tempting Christ,' by the same artist, is in good preservation, and with others exhibits an excellent old characteristic head, looking through short spectacles.

In this collection is a celebrated Carlo Dolce, 'Christ in Agony on the Mount,' with gilded rays ingeniously softened into a blue sky, and the blood dropping from his forehead on the grass, which is discoloured by it. It is the size of your two hands, and on copper, highly valued by the Genoese and others; but I confess that I have a distaste for the works of this hand (upon which I could enlarge a good deal), and cannot reconcile myself to this picture, even when the ladies were extolling its high finish (which I do not deny), its beauty, its affecting expression, and everything that is wonderful *in* it, and not in it.

Rubens, always striking, is here himself and his wife by his own hand, voluptuously indelicate, but splendid in colour and in style. He seems to have painted it in happy moments of slight inebriation. In the background is a bacchanalian figure holding a goblet of wine, and Cupid below completes the salacious idea. Rubens himself looks princely, is in armour, with a fur cap and feather.

But the finest thing in this collection is the portrait of a Chancellor in black robes, with open lace-worked collar hanging upon his shoulder. It is the thin head of a deep thinker, —listening and thinking; his dark intellectual eye looking through a pale reflecting face, with a serious severity of expression that rivets your attention. The head reminds me of the present Chancellor Manners of Dublin, who has one of the finest heads for a judge I ever saw. Perhaps, not so severe as this by Rubens, or so vigorous.

Was ever anything more like life?

But you are tired of the pictures at Genoa, which cannot boast of numerous *good* ones. There is a curious picture of the stoning of St. Stephen in the Church of St. Stephano alle Porte—the upper part of which is said to be by Giulio Romano, and the other by Raffaelle, the principal head having been destroyed by French soldiers. David has restored it unsuccessfully, as it is of a different colour and stone from the rest of the picture. The size is about ten feet by eight—on wood, and rather hard. But now I have done about pictures, I must say something about Genoese women, and so forth, to fill up my letter.

When an Englishman lands on the quay of Genoa, the variety of distinct smells of fruit and filth is very striking. One is surprised, too, by the odd foreign figures, the queer voices, the strange dresses, and the unusual expressions. A small, sallow, puny face is seen sunk in an immense hat, or, on the contrary, a large fleshy face like Liston's with a little brimless bonnet stuck on one side. The conversation, too, is so energetic, so loud, and there is so much action, the propriety of which, not knowing one word of the language, you cannot appreciate. You hurry through the narrow streets, passing people that seem to labour at each step, and are all fanning themselves, without distinction—men and women, young and old. Then you come to the corner of a street where they are preparing the picture of some Saint or Madonna, with lamps, and garlands, and crimson curtains, to be lighted up at night in great style, sometimes with illuminations and fireworks. And there are grand doings, where the women make assignations and the men meet their lovers. Then there is the horrible singing of casual voices, instead of the fine music which you expect in Italy. Nothing disappointed me so much as the singing of the general run of women. Instead of hearing full, capacious voices, harmonious if not educated, your ears are astounded with small, confined, pipy voices, powerless and squeaky; but I have no doubt that in society there may be some very different. The only powerful voice that I met with at Genoa (and she was allowed to be one of the best) was a Mrs. Barrie, an English lady, residing there.

At Genoa I heard of a sort of 'Beau Nash,' who, having a pretty good fortune, and being a well-whiskered fancy hero, amused himself by making his person as remarkable as his conceits and egotism were disagreeable and ridiculous. The Governor gives occasional grand balls in the winter, and generally sends his cards to the English in regular form, specifying, I believe, that it is a dress party. This Mr. ——, thinking of course the Genoese are so much inferior to him as an Englishman, treats them all with indifference, and accordingly goes to my Lord the Governor's ball dressed in top-boots, Belsher cravat, green riding coat, and white smalls, and dances away with his head upright and as dignified as if he were my Lord, with a *chapeau de bras* under his arm. He is fond of horses, and is, in fact, a groom, seldom seen out of his stable in the day, except when riding. He has a great deal of good things to say of every person known in Genoa, so that he entertains the ladies highly; for his wit, and the amusing way in which he tells his jokes, although personal, never fail to be his passport wherever he goes. He has besides a careless, fearless manner that serves him well; is a boxer of the first ring, and shows superior qualities as a rider.

The women of the country dress their heads without bonnets, and have a veil they call *mezzano*, a piece of muslin six or nine feet long, which they throw over the head, sometimes covering the face, and sometimes showing a little of the black hair, parted on the forehead, with occasionally a flash of the brightest and softest of eyes. This mezzano is worn with the greatest simplicity, and gives a grace and beauty that is truly magical; and if it chances to be worn by a beauty, the charm is irresistible. When the head turns the least, or tips to one side, what lines—what composition it gives! We see this in Raphael's pictures often. Although this muslin drapery or head-dress is worn by all classes in the morning, yet ladies of fashion and quality do not drive or promenade in the 'Aqua Sola' without the distinctive addition of a bonnet, which is made either of silk, gauze, or straw, exactly as they are worn in England at the present day. Indeed, there are so many English here that the fashions are soon transported. Black silk gowns are much worn, and being tied very tight at the waist, show the figure in all its fulness. It is the fashion here to be *embonpoint*, and the ladies feed themselves so that they become unnaturally stout. It is likewise the case at Florence and Rome. Their walk has more of majesty than any that I have seen. What an air! Milton must certainly have had the Italian women in his mind when he described the majesty of Eve.

Between Pisa and Florence there is a little beautiful town called Spezia, famous for its harbour, which is said to be the finest in the universe. I do not introduce the name of this place here for the purpose of mentioning its famous harbour, as I know nothing of these matters, but to observe to you that I saw one of the most beautiful women that ever was created, a divine face, in a servant-girl. I gazed at her for ten minutes with strained eyes and gaping mouth. She was in a shop talking to an old woman, and seemed rather pleased than otherwise at the attraction she exercised. What a model for a painter! In passing through Pisa I saw the Campo Santo with great interest, and regarded these works as the foundation of a school of design that prompted Raphael's great genius, and gave hints even to Michael Angelo.

I sketched a piece of the Holy Land that was brought from Jerusalem, and is kept sacred in this holy receptacle, likewise some plants that were growing on it, and some bits from the falling tower,—could I do less as a traveller?

I will write to Mr. Mayor, and tell him about Florence, as a continuation of this, which he will show you.

Although the following letter, to a certain extent, goes over some of the ground which the author had previously described, it is too interesting to be omitted:—

Rome, Sept. 28th, 1826.

My dear Sir,—Four or five months have now elapsed since the merry party from the Tees were separated on the Thames; and by some of that party, no doubt, many, many merry and happy hours have been laughed away in harmless mirth and pleasantry. It is a pleasure to me even at this distance—in so austere, so grave, so elevated, and so splendid a place as Rome—to remember the tricks and eccentricities, the buoyant enjoyments, the enthusiastic exultations, of the West End of Darlington,—not to forget the marine adventure and the 'Kitty awake' (as it was called)—the *aqua vita* turned so miraculously into vinegar (sour as *wargis*), like Billy Lackaday's small beer in the comedy. This brings me to mention my very tedious and unsocial passage from London to Genoa, a passage of six long weeks' duration, often becalmed for four or five days, sticking in the water like a log of wood, motionless, with nothing but a cloudless sky above, and the tiresome and painful monotony of a dazzling, glassy surface of water below—no object except, perhaps, the head of a sleeping tortoise at some distance, to break the immense expanse of shining waste, —sky-bounded. We had few books calculated to amuse us at sea. Veneroni's Italian Grammar and Exercises, with two or three more equally serious, became stupid, and are likely to cause a distaste for the same studies for some time to come. 'Aboard a ship' is not a 'seemly' place for study, except for a sailor, who is all the time in his element; but how few sailors study! If you recollect, you brought with you from Darlington 'An Essay on the Principles of Human Action,' or perhaps 'An Exposition of the

Sacraments,' which I believe you scarcely ever opened—perhaps from social excitement, a delightful hilarity, or more probably *ennui*, which, however, is a thing never known—a feeling never understood at the 'West End,' but banished like the plague or malaria, every means being taken to avoid or prevent it, as it should be; for what could we think of existence, wanting the beautiful simplicity and virtue of innocent enjoyment? But now I am prosing, and, if you please, we will change the subject and talk of something else.

I sit down to write, as much to endeavour to amuse you as to fulfil my promise of writing, without knowing where to begin, or what part to take, the best to meet my intentions—for my memory is glutted with objects so various, of such different interest, so important in the history of the world, and either of such vast magnificence in themselves, or of such interest in the associations they excite. Indeed, if we speak of Rome alone, at every step, every turn we take, we come upon some scene hallowed with its charm—possessed with its talisman, associated with the classics, important in history, or looking majestically through the eyes of venerable antiquity. On this subject, I must say, there is no end. However, as I know you are fond of excursions, and delight in the wonders of art and the beauties of nature, I will try to speak of what I saw at Tivoli, having made a visit there with a friend so late as yesterday, and the scenery being now fresh in my recollection, strong 'in my mind's eye.'

Although Tivoli is only three hours' drive from Rome, yet the road is so bad, uneven, and dusty, and the country so wanting in interest, that if you were not excited by the expectation of something at the end of your journey to repay you for all the hard thumps, and rubs, and shakes, and the constant action ' to and fro,' and from side to side, I am persuaded that most people would stop at the 'sulphur river,' which, smelling as it does, perhaps, ten times as strong as Middleton Spa, would complete the *finale* of disagreeables, and render the ' stop short' here memorable to the sensitive. The whole road (about eighteen miles), crossing the miserable and melancholy ' Campagna di Roma,' traverses a flat, uncultivated swamp, abounding in thistles, nettles, and every indigenous wild plant that adorns an abandoned or neglected soil, which, although having every appearance of capability, remains not only useless to man and animals, but, at certain seasons of excessive heat, is baneful and dangerous to the health and existence of both.

On our journey yesterday, I observed a long line of dense fog following the winding course of the Tiber, not like our mists upon similar rivers in England, thin, vaporous, and milky (as on the Skern), but a line of clouds, formed into regular and distinct cumuli—floating close, and extending only fifteen feet above the ground, so that we could see the tops of trees over their outlines; and on crossing the Tiber at half-past seven in the morning, a few miles from Rome, this fog was so thick as to prevent our seeing the figures of men and cattle that were meeting us upon the bridge, not more than forty or fifty feet from us. Had it not been for the noise of our carriage rumbling over the old arch some accident might have occurred (which although it might have come well in at this place as a 'bit of the romantic,' still we can do very well without by leaving it to the imagination); the bridge being narrow and admitting but one vehicle at a time to cross it. It is a genuine antique, untouched by the hand of the *restaurateur*, and the road is paved with irregularly-shaped, large flat stones, as was the custom in those days; their appearance when joined together resembling the map of England divided into its counties, each stone having its accidental or circumstantial division, which forms the exact counterpart to the boundary of the adjoining one; each line running as fantastical a course as the 'county line' or the windings of a river that sometimes serve for that purpose. The surface of this pavement is as unequally worn and torn as the outline of the stones is irregular, and subjects you to much exercise in leaps from your seat and thumps against your shoulders. I might here observe, that this taste for irregularity was possessed by the ancient Romans in other matters than pavements, for in their inscriptions on marble we see the writing undulating in crooked lines, running up to one corner, or down to another, some letters large, some small, words crowded and confused, and running one into another, or the contrary, the letters wide apart, large, and of unequal proportion. This apparent eccentricity sometimes excites a smile, and you would scarcely believe that a workman who had to labour over the cutting of a letter with tools, should not first mark out what he had to do, so as to get each letter and word in such a proper lineal situation as to be read with ease and facility; and this seems so simple and self-evident, that the irregularity could not be unintentional, but must have been the result of some perverse taste or fashion of the times, which was gratified by these crooked epitaphs and unruled lines.

Tivoli stands upon a rocky eminence commanding an extensive but barren view across the Campagna, bounded in the extreme distance by the Grand City! St. Peter's, breaking against the horizon, towers in the sky like a huge giant,—

> ' Whom transcendent glory raised
> Above his fellows!'

The inn at Tivoli is like most Italian inns;

it is characterised by a want of comfort and cleanliness, and all those nice little attentions to the wants and convenience of customers that make an English inn so pleasant and so tempting to visitors. This inn, although in a situation that is scarcely to be equalled as a temptation to the admirers of beautiful, romantic scenery, has nevertheless such indifferent accommodation that, if you are disposed to stop, you must look for private lodgings —which fortunately may be had. The town being considerable, and the scenery being attractive, strangers come and reside during summer and autumn, and the natives find it worth their while to fit up apartments to receive such visitors, who, being generally English, pay them well, or are expected to do so. Our breakfast at Tivoli was quite in the primitive style. Bread, eggs, and wine, with grapes and fresh butter, made up our fare; and that we might have something nice for dinner, we ordered a pigeon-pie! —a pigeon-pie! Could I avoid thinking of the exquisite, tender delicacy of such a dish at 'the West End,' for instance? I confess that, in my romantic and classical walk, with objects of the greatest interest, beauty, and novelty before me, the idea of 'this pigeon-pie' was ever crossing my mind; and after walking three or four hours, climbing rocks and zigzag roads, judge my disappointment when the pie was served on the table, with a darkbrown crust, thick, hard, and heavy, of a saturated drab-colour inside, with only *one* pigeon, for *two* hungry young travellers! It was what is called 'a standing pie,' and had a strong paste handle passing crescent-like from side to side like that of a tea-kettle. Could I but laugh when this piece of pastry was put on the table, with so much ceremony too, the cook looking in to see how it was received! It looked, indeed, so thumbed, so clumsy, so dark, and so odd, unrelieved by any of your modern attempts at ornament, that it could only have suited a person of very 'plain taste.' Yet our host thought, no doubt, that this was one of his 'crack dishes,' for he sent up to tell us what the expense of such a pie would be before he made it. This smacked of honesty, and showed that he did not wish us to be deceived.

THE FALLS.

From the window of our dining-room we had a beautiful view of a sweep of the river above the 'falls,' with rising banks topped with picturesque houses and turrets, with cattle, and figures of Italian peasant-women (washing clothes in the river), and one small fall of water, which serves as 'a prelude' to the scene. The constant roar and noise of falling waters, and the hollow sound of subterranean cataracts, make a wild and curious music to your repast, which, whilst at one moment it excites your imagination to poetic sublimity, subdues you again to calm reflection, or rouses impassioned thought.

From the same window (in the inn-yard) are seen the remains of a beautiful little circular temple, called 'the Temple of the Sibyl,' in tolerable preservation, and in proportion, symmetry, and situation exquisite; and if not the one copied by Claude, it is very similar to that introduced in many of his works (a circular temple with Corinthian pillars). Close to this, and nearly touching it, are seen portions of another temple of a square form, and dedicated to Vesta, but now formed into a church by modern brick walls, as unseemly as the idea is barbarous, and almost exceeding the story told of an Englishman who bought a round temple for the purpose of removing and placing it in his garden in England. The proper authorities, hearing of this circumstance, very judiciously ordered the money to be refunded to this tasteless Gothic barbarian, who would have robbed the rocky pinnacle of its temple, as he would have deprived the violet of its perfume, or the lily of its beauty, for the gratification of his own grovelling selfishness.

But let us descend to the bottom of the rock and see the 'first fall.' You hear it boiling and dashing its spray against the damp rocks. Halfway down the zig-zag path are seen two sons of nature (with moustachios wild), perched on a perpendicular eminence, sketching, with rapid hand and eye severe, the falling Anio, which, spitting its foaming mass, one hundred feet, sheer from its rocky bed into the dread abyss beneath, joins its other portion, long time lost, and tossed from rock to rock in subterranean darkness, as it rushes, howling and roaring, on its dreadful way, bringing animals or man disjointed or dashed piecemeal to the bottom, where you now are standing; wet with the spray, and deafened by the horrible noise. The cavern whence issues the subterranean fall is called 'the Grotto of Neptune,' and is extremely curious from its dark mysterious effect. In the morning, the prismatic colours are seen vividly reflected in the spray at the mouth of the Grotto. The fall here derives great advantage from the rocks, which are beautiful in colour and surface, and rise high and majestic in form. Next there are the Cascatelles (of Bernini the sculptor), who, bringing part of the river across the town of Tivoli for the use of its inhabitants, to drive their mills, and for other purposes, has thrown this part of the water over natural rocks in a singularly beautiful and striking way, so that from different points of view you get the most interesting and picturesque combinations. For instance, from one point, you see on the left, high up, the tower of a church; then in perspective you have the beautiful remains of the Villa of Mæcenas, or Villa d'Este; below these you have three waterfalls in perspective, the large one near to you falling and dividing itself in a most beautiful way, and the other two long streams rushing down a rocky slope; and again, in the distance, you can see Rome and St. Peter's. Another picture is seen the contrary way, looking up the river, taking in these falls differently varied, and the Villa of Catullus against the side of a hill which forms the boundary of the picture. The Villa of Horace might be taken in from another point. So that four or more capital pictures might be got, not only of beautiful and romantic scenery, but of objects that excite classical associations. Now we cannot have such objects united with the falls either of Tees or Clyde, both which appear to me tame and bare after Tivoli. I have not seen Terni, but I am told it is superior to Tivoli in grandeur and extent.

On our return from Tivoli, we visited the ruins of Adrian's Villa, which is calculated as much as anything to give a splendid idea of the magnificence of the ancient Romans. The masses and piles of building, consisting of the

Imperial palaces, theatre, baths, barracks for the Prætorian guard, stables, &c., occupy about as much extent as the town of Darlington. The situation, too, is beautiful, and the grounds are embellished with large pines and cypress-trees; but the plough now finds its way into the halls and courtyards, and turns up pieces of marble and lumps of wall, that cover the surface wherever you go. The remains of the Baths of Caracalla (which are near Rome) give an idea of buildings upon a larger scale, and are magnificent in themselves, exciting (as the relics of greatness generally do) at once astonishment and melancholy.

I might continue to any length with the ruins of ancient Rome now existing, but of guide-books and tours of Italy you have plenty, describing everything that is, and much that is not. I must now close this confused packet by asking what I am to do for you? Here are Tivoli, Terni, Frascati, Ruins of Rome, all subjects of intrinsic value and deep interest. Let me do you something a little larger than the last.

I have had an interview with the *major-domo* of the Pope, and have succeeded in getting permission to study in the Sistine Chapel, from those stupendous works of Michael Angelo. You may judge of the scale of the objects when I tell you that the canvas I have ordered for one figure of a Prophet is eleven feet high, and this only takes in one figure from the top of the head to the feet, and the prophet is sitting.

It is my most anxious wish to obtain copies of all the best of Michael Angelo's works that are in this chapel, as they are decidedly superior to anything of epic composition in existence; and indeed they are so tremendous in power and grandeur, that no one has hitherto attempted so arduous an undertaking. I must erect a scaffolding from forty to fifty feet high to enable me to finish them. Then, again, there was some difficulty in obtaining permission just now, which my letter from Sir Thomas Lawrence cleared away, and I found no obstruction to my wishes. I have a beautiful figure of Eve, and two other smaller commissions, to do for Sir Thomas in this chapel.

To Sir Thomas Lawrence.   Rome, Oct. —, 1826.

Sir,—You were kind enough to request me to write to you from Rome, so soon as I should have seen the Sistine Chapel, and put in progress the copies you did me the honour to commission me to make from those stupendous works of Michael Angelo. You likewise spoke of a select set of copies of these glorious things, which had long been the object of your solicitude, as you wished to propose them to the Royal Academy.

The idea of getting large copies of the Prophets, Sibyls, and some others, seems to excite expectations of pleasure in the breasts of every one; and the thought of the Royal Academy of London possessing such copies would be much for the interest of the British school, and on a task of such a nature I should enter with all the enthusiasm that the magnificence of the subject would inspire. The expense of such a set of copies would be comparatively trifling to an institution like that of the Royal Academy. At any rate, in the projection of a new building, it might be of importance to bear them in mind.

Through the influence of your letter to Sig. P. Camuccini, I have obtained permission to study in the Chapel; but as I can only be there for three weeks, by reason of ceremonies that take place in it from the end of October to the beginning of April, it will be enough for me to rub in carefully the proportions, colour, and effect from below, and then finish them from a scaffolding which I am promised in the spring, when I can have three months without interruption of any kind.

There has been some noise lately about persons having taken tracings from the 'Last Judgment,' and imaginary injuries were mentioned. So that I found, in a conversation with Mr. Morris at Florence, that permission at all would be difficult, if not impossible, to obtain. It appears, however, that the *major-domo* is only directed to be more particular in consequence, and that propriety of conduct must gain indulgence for the future.

Of the portion of the 'Last Judgment' that has been cleaned by the simple process of rubbing with bread, there are two or three opinions about. Some say it is spoiled, others that it might have been. The colouring of the flesh in the angels, coming as it does against a deep blue sky, takes much of the richness of Titian. The figures seem no longer attached to the background, but are suspended in the air, floating along the azure blue with masterly foreshortening, and, in this part, certainly not without grace and an attention to aerial perspective that is not perceived through the obscure opacity that wraps as a cloud the other dingy portions.

Allow me to return my sincere thanks for your kindness in sending me the two letters, and believe me ever,

Your obliged, and obedient servant,

WM. BEWICK.

I have commenced with the upper part of the Sibylla Delphica for you on a canvas six feet high, which takes in the figure below the knee, the two hands with two boys behind. It is on a scale larger than life, but not quite so large as the original. The head has much of beauty as well as powerful expression; and you may depend upon my endeavours to make the copy worth your recollections of the sublime original.

The Prophet Jeremiah, too, is begun, the full size of the fresco, on a canvas eleven feet high. After finishing the outline with dark colour, the size and grandeur of the proportions were quite striking when near the eye. In these figures each head is upon a scale of about two English feet.

CHAPTER II.

MR BEWICK'S ILLNESS — LANDLADY WITH A GLASS EYE — LADY WESTMINSTER — TABLEAUX VIVANTS — MRS. CHENIE — LIVING IN ROME — SCOTCH AND ENGLISH IN ROME — WILKIE — THE HOLY WEEK — EASTER SUNDAY — MAGNIFICENT PROCESSION — THE CARNIVAL — PRACTICAL JOKING — THE FUN OF CARNIVAL — MASKED BALL.

IN the latter part of this year, as may be seen from the previous letters, we find Mr. Bewick in Rome, and, amid all the novelty and interest of the scenes by which he was surrounded, eager for news from home. The marble palaces, the gorgeous processions, the magnificent art-collections of the Eternal City, could not efface the feeling with which he looked back to familiar Darlington, and the relatives he had left there. By this time he was diligently at work in the Sistine Chapel, where, partly from mischance, and partly through his own imprudence, he contracted an illness which must have interfered greatly with the manual practice of his art.

Wilkie, too, was in Rome at the same time, and visited him. This great artist, who was in a very indifferent state of health, must have had a high opinion of his friend Bewick, for we find him urging him to attempt the production of some large and important painting for exhibition in London. The following letter to his sister gives some account of his life and doings in Rome, but says little or nothing of the impressions made upon him by that city and its magnificent remains of antiquity.

Rome, Dec. 11th, 1826.

My dearest Bess,—I received your letter yesterday, so that it has been two months coming to me, for it is dated 10th of October. I suspect it has been in the Post-office here for five weeks, in consequence of your putting 'Post Restante,' upon it, which I must beg you not to do again, but direct for me at Freeborn, Smith, and Co., Rome, and the letter will come direct without being detained. You do not mention if Mr. Smith has received a letter from me, nor if Tom had got his. I have been very impatient at not hearing from you, or some of the family, so long. Your two letters are the only ones I have had since I left England, except some from London; and a letter from Darlington is very acceptable at this distance. You might write twice as much in your letter if you wrote closely and took time; begin a few days before you send it, and write a little every day, so that you will forget nothing that would amuse or interest me at this distance. You must forgive me if I write ill-naturedly in this letter, for I am not in a good humour, nor inclined to be good-natured. The reason is, that I have a pain in my right hand that tortures me at every turn of the pen; and it concerns me much when I have to tell you that for two months I have not been free from pain in some part of my body, for whilst I was working very hard, and perhaps perspiring in the 'Capello Sistino,' the windows were set open to get rid of the smell of the paint, and most unfortunately, in consequence, I caught a rheumatism, which, beginning at my left shoulder, has jogged on from part to part, until it is now in my right foot and right hand. These are, I hope, the last places it can creep to, and I trust now soon to be able to resume my labours. When it came to my knees I could not sleep at nights, but passed a most wretched time. I write with considerable difficulty, my right hand being swollen and very painful. The doctor has ordered me to put half-a-dozen leeches upon it, which I shall do to-morrow. My mother will know well what an attack of this kind is. Thank God, I am now almost quite recovered, which it gives me great pleasure to tell you.

The weather here has been for some time wet and damp, and we have had one shower of hail — the hailstones as large as filberts, and coming against the windows like marbles. There has been no snow in Rome, but we see it on the mountains. The winter so far has been like our spring at Darlington, rather cold, but no ice, and I have four roses in a glass in my room as beautiful as in summer. In consequence of my cold I have been but to one party this winter, which was given by the Countess of Westmoreland, and was very gay. The English here, who in winter are numerous, keep up a style of fashion and gaiety which becomes the reputation they have of being very rich and extravagant, and indulging in unnecessary luxuries, and the Italians say, 'that we have carpets even upon our stairs,' which is a luxury they cannot see the good of, besides that it costs so much money.

Mr. Bewick remained settled in Rome during the year 1827, extending his circle of acquaintance, enlarging his knowledge of life, and to a certain extent entering into the gaieties of the city. His introductions procured him admission to a society in every way congenial to his taste, Rome being the centre, not only of a considerable colony of artists, but also of persons of rank and fashion, the majority of whom took a deep interest in artists and their works. Much attention was paid to him by families of distinction, and he gladly availed himself of such opportunities as he had of becoming acquainted with the world of rank and fashion. If a too ready attention to the claims of society is considered, on the one hand, inconsistent with the laborious practice of art, on the other hand it has the advantage of enlarging the artist's knowledge of life, and rendering him familiar with the manners and customs of a class on whom his success is so largely dependent.

Mr. Bewick unfortunately still suffered from the attack to which allusion has been previously made. For several months he was compelled to submit to the treatment of a patient, and appears to have suffered greatly from rheumatic pains, the consequence of the exposure to atmospheric influences to which he had unfortunately submitted. Still, though his right hand was greatly affected, he was able both to work at his easel, and to enter into the pleasures of society, though doubtless he could do neither with so much devotion as in other circumstances might have been expected of him.

The following letters to Mrs. Bewick continue the record of his life in Rome :—

Rome, January 29th, 1827.

My dear Friends at Home,— Your two letters with the bill came safe. They had evidently been opened and sealed up again. This, I suppose, was done at the Post Office at Darlington, a practice long common there, which, no doubt, will ere long receive its due punishment. You say that I have told you nothing about Rome, but as you can read in guide-books and travels more than I could tell you in a letter, it will be more interesting to write you anything connected with myself, which such books cannot possibly tell you. Besides, out of the few months I have been here, three have been consigned to racking pains, swellings, and rubbings with ointments, wrapping-up with flannels, bleeding, bathing, and physicking, and the devil knows what of disagreeables; for I have had a landlady with a glass eye, and if ever there was a fiend in the shape of a woman, this is one. She annoyed me constantly, although she had nothing to do with me, for I had my own apartments and my man-servant, but still she continued to draw from me daily a torrent of invective better unspoken. I have now got out of her house, a little Irishman having taken the lodging of me; and I am glad to say she has already received such a tearing, and swearing, and stamping from this little Irishman, that she will not like to come much where he is. He says she is extremely humble and good-natured since he kicked her out of his studio; but he knew how she had annoyed me, and was determined to take the first opportunity to pay her off; for he is a fine-spirited little fellow, and, like his countrymen, easily put into a fury of passion. The reason of my moving was that I could not do anything for myself, not even cut my own meat or tie my cravat; and I found it necessary to go where I should be taken care of and nursed. So I took the lodging which I first came to, and made a bargain for board and everything; and I must say that it is owing to the care and attention of both landlord and landlady that I am able to write this letter, for my right hand has not been uncovered for a month, and it is with some difficulty that I guide the pen, my fingers not having their proper strength or flexibility.

As to painting or drawing, I have not done anything since my right hand has been covered up, so that I have seen little of the winter's gaiety in Rome. Last week Lady Westmoreland sent her carriage for me, to give my assistance in the preparations she is making for a grand dress-ball, which will take place on the 12th of February. All the ambassadors and great people from all countries are to be present; and there will be music and dancing, and all kinds of splendour and gaiety. You

TABLEAUX VIVANTS. 39

will say that I cannot dance, or play music, or sing; and what can I be wanted for? I will tell you. During the evening there will be exhibited what are called *tableaux*, which are no more than people dressed up to represent the different characters in some celebrated picture. They are placed behind a gold-frame in the positions and with the expressions of the picture. A green cloth is put all round the frame, and hides the light or anybody that may be behind. Then a piece of thin black gauze is thrown over the front of the frame, and the effect is perfectly beautiful. There are several of these pictures made during the evening, in which the noblemen and ladies, and people of fashion, stand for the characters; I mean such as have faces and figures adapted for it. The character that I have to take has been twice rehearsed. The subject is a young warrior, dressed in steel armour, and his page is buckling on his shoulder-piece. A young lady of exquisite beauty is to be the page. Her lovely face and delicate hands will be set off to great advantage by my grim visage, for I am to frown most abominably. Lady Westmoreland calls out, 'Frown, Mr. Bewick! frown, Sir! You must look cross for once, for this is your page only—you must not think she is a pretty girl.'

This is the first piece that has been tried, and those who were placed as judges exclaimed, ' Beautiful! wonderful effect!' and so on. One gentleman, a sculptor, not thinking at the time how it was produced, called out, ' How wonderfully like nature!' Another, a painter, came very close with his friend, and, not knowing that the lady was an Englishwoman and understood their conversation, said, ' How very like flesh her face is!' and then thinking she was an Italian added, ' A devilish pretty girl that page is!' While we were standing so, my page whispered to me that she should not be able to stand still or keep from laughing if those people were to talk, so I gave the signal, and the folding-doors were closed. Just as this was done and I was putting off the armour, we were told that a lady had arrived to see us, and the picture was made up again. After this I walked into the party with the armour on. As it was taken off, the ladies laughed heartily at the odd figure that the removal of each piece made me look, some comparing the process to the shelling of a lobster, others to the peeling of an orange.

The lady who arrived late, and whose taste seemed to be held in high esteem, requested to be introduced to me; and she told me that she belonged to Newcastle, and knew T. Bewick, the 'celebrated engraver.' This lady is Mrs. Chenie, widow of General Chenie. I have paid her a visit, and was shown some of her drawings and paintings, which are quite exquisite. She is a true artist, and is drawing and painting every day of her life. She is, besides, a most accomplished woman, and lives in high state here with her family. Her daughter dressed herself in her Carnival dress to show it us. The Carnival (which you will read of in books of travels) takes place here in about twenty days. They will have me dressed in a splendid Greek costume to go to the masque-ball given by the Duke di Bracciano during Carnival. The Baron Stackelberg is to lend me this costly dress; and although this is a sort of thing that I do not like, yet I will go, because I shall see a great deal that is new to me, and curious, and in fact it is one of the things that everybody comes to see.

Now to answer your letters. I am sorry to hear of Mr. S.'s fever, and of my mother being ill. You must nurse her and take care of her, for there is no one, next to yourself, that I more esteem or love. I am glad you had such a pleasant and quiet Christmas, and that you drank my health on my birthday. You never mention Sister Ann, I suppose she never writes to Darlington. The Christmas here was very gay, but I saw nothing of the gaiety. The processions and illuminations are very fine, I am told. The people here, particularly the women, are very idle and dirty, and half their time seems to be spent in festas, and holidays, and religious ceremonies, that are of very little good, I am afraid, if any. At ten o'clock at night Rome is as quiet as Blackwell, and everybody asleep, except those who have parties. There are no rows or quarrelling in the streets, no drunkenness, and no watchmen or guards of the night.

Your letter came too late for me to keep your birthday; however, I will keep it with a friend or two. I wish you were here to mend my pen, for your letters were written so nicely, and, though close, I had no difficulty in reading them. An Italian gentleman, seeing one on the table, observed how beautifully it was written, and with what small characters. As to my return to Darlington you know everything depends upon my health. I cannot determine upon anything until I am quite well. I am quite persuaded that the atmosphere of Rome does not agree with me, but people say everybody is ill at first arrival, and that after this I shall not feel it.

I long to taste your mince-pies. We have no cakes here except plum-cake, which is bought at the shops. I have excellent wine for twopence-halfpenny a bottle. Bread is about half the price that you pay. For a capon or large fowl we pay about fifteen or eighteen-pence; but then they are larger than yours. Then we have wild boar's flesh, which is delightful, and cocks-combs'; and they make me every day five or six different dishes to dinner, although one of them would be enough. But I sometimes make a clear board.

Mr. Wilkie is still here, in delicate health, but not ill. Two dinners have been given to him as testimony of his talent, one by twelve English students, and the other by all the Scotch people in Rome. The second arose out of pique at the first dinner. I was one of the twelve of the first entertainment, and now there is a feeling of ill-will between the Scotch and English. An English lady has written the following lines on the Scotch dinner :—

> ' To give Wilkie a dinner the Scots have decreed,
> So in praises and eating he 's honour'd indeed ;
> But to order his pictures they never found need —
> 'Tis enough that he 's born on the north of the Tweed.'

It was Wilkie's own assertion that he never had received one commission from Scotland.

I am glad you keep up your French and music ; remember me to all friends.

It is pleasing to learn of that fine benevolent gentleman the Rev. Dalton, of Croft, and his amiable family being so highly spoken of for their attention and kindness to the poor people in the parish. I find I have told you nothing about Rome— its grandeur, its ruins, and its filth ; but I will tell you something in my next letter if there is room for it.

Yours,
WILLIAM BEWICK.

From Rome, January 29th, 1827.

During the Holy Week Mr. Bewick's attention was almost unavoidably distracted from the labours which usually occupied his time by the novel spectacles and magnificent ceremonies of which Rome at that period is the scene. The magnificent displays which take place in the Sistine Chapel at that time compelled him to remain idle for some days, and thus he had leisure to gaze with others on those pompous shows by which the Church of Rome exercises so great an influence over certain minds. On Easter Sundays St. Peter's Church is a spectacle of unexampled splendour; and an observant artist could not but be struck by the ingenuity displayed in the arrangement of ceremonies naturally so well calculated to carry away the feelings of the unreflecting worshipper. Nor was he less disposed to take his part in the pleasures which follow those ably directed manifestations of devotion. His health now considerably improved, he was able to enter into the amusements of masquerade and Carnival—species of entertainment which, with his hearty, joyous disposition, he was in every way disposed to enjoy, as we may see by the following letter he addressed to his sister:—

Rome, April 13th, 1827.

My Dearest Bess,—I only received your letter three days ago, although it is dated so far back as Feb. 26th, and I think you had better direct to me at No. 30 Via del Gambero, 3 Piazzo, Rome,—and then, perhaps, I may get it sooner. Your letter amuses me much, although I think you might have written more. Mary, too, is very kind in adding her mite of amusement to me. I see you all in Darlington when I read your letters, and am glad to see you so— all in good health and spirits—as I suppose you are when you say nothing to the contrary. I am glad that I can say, too, that I am quite well, can cut my dinner and clip my moustachios with my right hand. I have been working at the Sistine Chapel, but stopped for some days on account of the Holy Week, during which the chapel is occupied with daily ceremonies. Palm Sunday was the beginning—the blessing the palms by the Pope—which, although not so splendid and pompous as the ceremonies on

Easter Sunday, yet was interesting, and the singing beautiful, but Easter Sunday eclipsed everything in splendour and magnificence. The whole body of the Church of St. Peter's, and the square in front, was one immense crowd; and when the Pope came out at a window in front of the Church to bless the people, it was such a sight as I never saw. There seemed to be a world of people, and although the weather was rainy, all Rome and the country around appeared to be there; the umbrellas, too, adding much to the effect. Every eye was raised to the window, and when the Pope came all the soldiers and individuals there took off their hats and fell down upon their knees in the most profound reverence to receive the blessing; this, too, in front of a building the extent and magnificence of which is the admiration and wonder of the world.

In the evening the whole of this building, even up to the cupola and cross, was to have been completely covered and illuminated with lamps, and at a short distance, at the Castle of St. Angelo were to be displayed some splendid fireworks. All this the bad weather has prevented. The ceremonies at Easter are splendidly beautiful—the dresses of the Pope and the Cardinals are magnificent, and the procession in the Church of St. Peter's exceeds anything of the kind I ever saw or imagined. The Pope, too, looked better than I have seen him. He is brought from the altar on that day into the centre of the church on a chair covered with crimson and gold, which is carried on the shoulders of twelve men, eight more carrying a canopy over his head, all dressed in crimson-figured damask. The Cardinals were in their robes of white and gold, scarlet and purple, some carrying the mitres of the Pope all embossed with precious stones. There were two Greek priests that were quite magnificent. Then followed the Pope's body-guard, all formed of the young nobility, and very handsome men. The Pope, after being taken from his chair, kneels and prays in the centre of the Church, and so do all the people; then the relics of our Saviour are shown from a balcony, and all the people cross themselves; and after this the Pope is taken in procession to the balcony-window in front of the Church to bless the people. He throws from the window two printed papers, which are called bulls, and for which the people scramble and fight to see who can get them.

But I must now tell you something of the Carnival. To tell you the truth, I really enjoyed it—I suppose the more from having been confined so much in the house previously, and I think the excitement and gaiety really did me a world of good, for everybody in Rome, of all ages and conditions, was merry, and the laughing and feasting continued for eight days, with all sorts of fun and antics—the people dressed in all sorts of curious dresses—with all sorts of odd faces and masques of strange expression. The sport begins about one or two o'clock, when all the world comes out into the principal streets, either on foot or in carriages—or to the windows and balconies, which are all covered with crimson or green damask. The principal street, which is called the Corso, and where everything is in uproar and frolic, has a beautiful effect with these long damask cloths hanging from the windows, all full of people gaily dressed, throwing comfits at those below whom they recognise on foot or in carriages. Sometimes handbattles are fought with these comfits, particularly when two carriages rest opposite each other, and the parties are known to each other. These battles are generally fought by the English. You will scarcely believe that in two hours seventy pounds of comfits were thrown from the carriage I was in, and there were only four of us; but we certainly fought some hard battles.

One day the carriage stopped opposite a barber's shop, and seeing a poor fellow sitting to be shaved, with his chin all soap, we involuntarily threw our bullets all together in at the door, which was open, and the shop was presently covered with them (they are made, not of sugar, but paste or lime). The barber and the man to be shaved ran away, the latter covering his eyes with his hands, the soap upon his chin, and his mouth full of comfits (for he began to speak when he saw us throwing); it was quite a hailstorm. Everybody is mad at this time, and there is no economy or reserve. Some throw kisses made of sugar, and others flowers. This fun continues till an hour before dark, when the guns fire as a signal for the carriages to move off the street.

A horse-race takes place immediately after, and the soldiers clear the road for it. This racing is not like an English horse-race, for the horses are made to run *without riders*, which may appear odd to you. They are started at one end of the street and run to the other, having tin goads, with sharp points to prick and goad them, attached to their sides and backs. The horses are poor creatures, no better than our worst cart-horses, neither trained, nor fed, nor bred for a race. In the evenings there are masqued balls at the theatres, where everybody goes dressed as he fancies, in masque or not. This is the long-expected and delightful time for the ladies, who either go to intrigue themselves, or to watch their husbands or lovers, who are generally known to them, even if they be masqued. This is, indeed, the grand time for making love, and is looked forward to with anxious expectation. You must know that the men and women speak through the mouth of the masque with an altered squeaking voice that rarely can be distinguished, and I was completely deceived myself. A masque came to me and conversed with me some time. I made up my mind who it was, and walked the whole evening at intervals with him, talking of a variety of private matters that he seemed to know, and he kept up the thing so well that I was satisfied he was an English friend, and we agreed to sup together with two or three more. After all was over, we went to supper, all being masqued but myself; and while we sat and chatted, waiting for supper, my companion told me he was not the person I took him for. The others all guessed who he was, each taking him for a different person, and when he took off his masque we were all completely astonished to find him quite a different person from what we had supposed. The laughter was tremendous, for he turned out to be an American, a young man all knew very well without the masque. Yes, the fun of Carnival is certainly capital. People of all sorts come to you, torment and teaze you to death, and say anything they like; the women perhaps being worse than the men.

The masque ball that I mentioned to you given by the Duke of Bracciano was splendid beyond description, all the beauty and fashion of Rome being there. My dress attracted universal attention and admiration; and I will

MAMELUKE DRESS.

describe it to you for your amusement. It was a true Mameluke dress, just brought from Egypt by a French gentleman. The costume was complete and unique, and I have sat to two painters who have made pictures of me in it. The under-dress was a sort of long jacket of rich striped shining silk of a peculiar bright scarlet, with blue and white, and the sleeves tightly buttoned from the wrist to the elbows, with small silk buttons attached to cord. Over this came another jacket of the same material, with loose sleeves hanging open below the tips of the fingers. Then came the wide trousers of green cloth, of a rich russet colour, like a russet apple, made like a very wide petticoat, sewed at the bottom with two holes for the feet. Wrapped five or six times round the waist was a cincture of striped silk, fringed at the ends, in which was stuck an antique silver-hafted, short Turkish sword. Then came the short outer jacket, of the same colour as the trousers, all ornamented with gold, and the long sword hanging by a gold cord. Light yellow morocco boots, turned up at the points, and a white turban, with the throat uncovered, completed the costume.

When I entered the rooms I was stopped by the Duke and Duchess, who wished to examine my dress, as it was so perfectly elegant and rich, and my head so completely Eastern —with my black mustachios, bare neck, and not a bit of hair to be seen on the head — that they exclaimed, 'Superb! superb!' As I did not expect this, you may easily suppose how glad I was to get out of so conspicuous and trying a situation. But when I had slipped into the more crowded rooms, I perceived that the Duchess had brought the Duke of Hamilton to see my dress. Wilkie was arrayed in a splendid costume, for which I believe he had been at a considerable expense; mine cost me nothing. There was a capital masque at this ball, an English gentleman dressed one side as a man, and the other as a woman,—the latter he called his *better half*. He spoke with one side of his mouth like a lady, and with the other with a rough voice like a man.

Lady Westmoreland continues to give *tableaux*, and I am in want of money. Send to me by return of post, in the same way as you did before. I dined with a friend on Sunday, on lamb and green peas; lamb is $1\frac{3}{4}d.$ per lb. Remember me to all the family, and believe me,

Yours,
WILLIAM BEWICK.

Direct to me, Via del Gambero, 30 Piazzo, Rome.

The weather has been rather wet for a few days, and I feel my right hand and foot inclined to twinges of rheumatism, but I hope the hot sun will take it away again.

CHAPTER III.

ERECTION IN THE SISTINE CHAPEL—APPROACH OF SUMMER—OPERA BY A LADY—TWO UNFORTUNATE FRIENDS—FONTANA DELLA DEA EGERIA—CHAPEL OF THE MADONNA—EXCURSION IN THE NEIGHBOURHOOD OF ROME—ALBANO—THE CAFFE AT RICCIA—THE GERMAN ARTIST ON HIS TRAVELS—VILLAGE OF GENTANO—BATHS OF NOCERA—PLEASANT ENTERTAINMENT—A STORM.

PARTLY, no doubt, through his illness during the winter, and partly through the uncertainties and difficulties that beset the artist in the early part of his career, Mr. Bewick was still unable to depend on his own exertions entirely, and, to provide for the expenses of his residence in Rome, was compelled to apply to his father for assistance. The work on which he was engaged in the Sistine Chapel rendered necessary the erection of a large scaffolding, an expensive work, but which was indispensable to the task which he had undertaken. As the summer months approached, bringing with them heat and the dread of malaria, the English visitors took their flight from Rome, and the now comparatively solitary artist began to find his residence in it dull and weary. But he had come for a certain purpose, which he believed to be essential to his success as an artist, and till that purpose was accomplished, he determined not to return to England. Gibson, the sculptor, was one of the most valued friends whom Bewick made in Rome. The painter always speaks in the highest terms of his brother artist, and Gibson was no less sincere in his appreciation of Bewick, as will be seen in more than one place in the course of this correspondence.

Rome, June 2nd, 1827.

My dear Friends at Home,—It is nearly two months since I wrote to you, telling you that I was in want of money, and as I have not had an answer, I have drawn a bill upon my father for twenty pounds, which will come to Darlington for his acceptance, and you will arrange with Backhouse's people where it will be made payable : I suppose, at Hammersley's, in London, will be the best. I should have waited your letter with patience, but that my winter's illness has not only wasted my time, but cost me a good deal of extra expense; and again, I have had a very high scaffolding put up at the Sistine Chapel, which has cost me a good deal, but it was indispensable for the works I am engaged upon. I am glad to tell you that my health is perfectly recovered, and that I hope to be able to remain in Rome during the summer, working hard, to make up for lost time in the winter; but you may rely upon it that, if I feel the slightest indications of the fever, I will go into the country immediately, and not return till the danger is quite over. The heat has not been very great yet; indeed, I have felt very little difference between this and London, and I think it equally hot in May. The weather has been very changeable, frequent rains, and cloudy, as in England. This is usual in this climate. I cannot say that I like Rome much, and were it not for the purpose for which I came, I should not stop; but as I have come so far I am determined to do what I came to do, if my health will carry me through, which I sincerely hope it will, now that I have gone so far. The hot weather seems to agree with me the best. It is the wet and damp that puts me out, and I still feel pangs of rheumatism in my right hand when there is wet; but I have great hopes that the perspiration by the excessive heat of summer may completely rid me of what gives me not a little anxiety. The English visitors have nearly all left Rome, and it is a very dull place.

Mr. Sams, who was here about a fortnight, is gone to Sicily and Egypt, but expects to be at Darlington in about seven or eight months. He was quite a figure here, and was described to me before I saw him in a way that made me laugh. He came to me at the Sistine Chapel, and looked very well, with a white hat and clean gloves. He came up to the top of the scaffolding, and climbed all the ladders with great caution. He gave me three oranges, and wished me all good luck.

I have not heard from Robert, or Thomas, or anybody—neither have I written. What you told me about the expense of postage prevented me, and I think it very prudent, for so long as all is going on well, we cannot but feel satisfied. However, I pray you always to write me all you can about them—and my sister Ann, you must not forget to remember me to her. I suppose Mary is quite accomplished upon the pianoforte, and other lady-like qualifications. I am glad to hear she was the belle of the ball, and that you yourself enjoyed it so much. By-the-bye there is a young Italian lady here who has composed an opera, the music of which (to my taste) is very sweet and melodious. She is called for upon the stage every evening after the curtain drops, and is applauded by all the gentlemen— the ladies seem not to be moved—perhaps they are a little jealous. She seems very modest and lady-like, and it is remarkable that this is the first opera that has been written by a lady—it is no less curious than true. Ladies write novels, poetry, and history, paint pictures, and make statues, and act plays, but never write music or compose operas. This last is a great undertaking, so many instruments to attend to, and such variety of expression required.

Two young friends of mine, who came about the same time as myself, have been extremely unfortunate here. One I knew before in London. He came to the Cappello Sistino to draw with me, and I suppose the whole thing, being so grand and so extensive, overpowered him. After finishing one drawing, he went to bed in the evening, and felt something at his breast. Presently the blood flowed out of his mouth in a most dreadful way; and when the doctors were sent for, they said he had broken a blood-vessel, which they thought arose from over-anxiety. He is now a great deal better. The young gentleman is a Scotchman, of most respectable parents and connexions. He has been, and is now, confined to his room, his mind having become deranged; and all I could get him to say was that he had acted imprudently, and spent all his money at Florence, and could not submit to explain matters to his family. He cannot have spent much money, for he was always a most prudent young man, as the Scotch people in general are. It is true he visited the best society, but this costs little.

I have had two busts done of me, one by the first English sculptor here. I shall preserve a cast for you, and send it over, or bring it; better to send it. His name is Gibson, a fine, simple-minded, clever genius, with a very refined and poetical taste, and devoted to his art. He tells me all that he lives for is to leave some fine works to posterity. He is very attentive to me, and we walk almost every evening, talking of art, and the fine antique statues. There is a fine grotto (called the Fontana della Dea Egeria). This grotto, according to Flaminius Vacca, was consecrated by Numa Pompilius to the wood-nymph Egeria. At the upper end of it was found a recumbent statue called Egeria. This statue is in very good style, but, the upper part being naked, it is easy to perceive that it is a male figure, perhaps a river-god. The grotto, being in ruins, is picturesque. It likewise appears from classic writers that the fountain of Egeria was near the ancient Porta Capena; but we have no good authority for calling the fountain in question that of Egeria.

There is another interesting edifice, which is about one mile from Rome, called the Chiesa di S. Agnese fuori di Porta Pia. The Chapel of the Madonna contains a beautiful antique candelabrum, and a head of our Saviour by Michael Angelo. Beauty of form and depth of expression are so rarely met with in Michael Angelo, that this may not only be said to be one of his happiest efforts, but the finest instance of power, sensibility, and elevated character to be met with in the heads of Christ. There is a touch of sorrow with dignity, an eye of affliction, deep-sunk, serene, and beautiful. It is most highly finished, wonderfully simple of style, fleshy, and exempt from any appearance of mannerism. It seems just taken from the chisel of the artist, it is so fresh.

You must tell me about the additional piece of garden ground you wish to buy. How is my dear mother, and my father? I suppose he still goes on with the geography. Tell him we have green peas, and beans, and strawberries, and cherries, the same as in his garden, and the country looks beautiful; but there seems to me to be a great want of green grass-fields, which are so luxuriant and so delightful in England. The thorn, too, is wanting in May with its fragrance, but there is instead the perfume of the orange-blossom and the lemon-tree, and other luxuriant flowering trees. The people here regularly go to bed in the middle of the day, now that the weather is getting hot, and the fashionables do not get up in the morning before twelve or one, sometimes two. Visits are made in the evening, and the theatres are not over before half-past twelve or one. Remember me to Mr. Smith's family, Mr. Botcherby, and all those who are kind enough to inquire after me. My brother John, how does he do? And Tom, is there any talk of his getting a wife? You need not send anything to Newcastle.

My dear Bess, yours truly,

W. BEWICK.

In the following letter we find an interesting record of an excursion which Mr. Bewick took to some places in the neighbourhood of Rome :—

Rome, July 22nd, 1827.

MY DEAR BESS,— Your long-expected letter arrived two days ago, and I am much obliged to you for sending me so much news. It gives me great pleasure to hear the most trifling thing that you do, or that is going on at home. You cannot write me too much of this sort of news. With regard to the copyhold or life-rents, as you do not explain to me, I cannot advise you; but you cannot do better than follow your own judgment, and I am quite satisfied if you are on the spot all will be right, for I have great reliance upon your prudence. If the purchase is thought a good one, you can make an investment. The only thing is that I do not know what money I may want, as I am not certain of receiving regular remittances from Sir Thomas Lawrence, and therefore at this time you must not make large purchases, although desirable; but I will leave all to yourself. I am at much more expense than usual on account of the scaffolding, and other outlay connected with the large work I am doing.

You do not tell me how Jane's love affair comes on; and what is Tom doing with his lady love? and dear Molly, how does she do? My father too, has he been busy with his garden this spring? My mother is very kind in wishing me home before the cold weather; but she must remember that I have not been able to do anything during the winter, and that the summer is the only time I can have the scaffolding put up in the Sistine Chapel. Even now, when it was thought that nothing would be done in it at all, I am obliged to leave off for a fortnight, on account of the making of two Cardinals. This not only wastes my time, but costs me ten crowns besides. Thus I hope you will not make me more impatient by urging me to come, when I have so much vexation and require so much patience to enable me to remain to finish, as I am determined to do, if possible. I intend to try to remain in Rome during the summer.

Two days ago I felt rather unwell, and I am so afraid of the fever that I went into the country immediately, to a friend at a village, about twelve miles from Rome, called Albano, which is situated upon the side of a mountain where the air is healthy. I arrived there to a breakfast of goat's-milk and eggs; after which we went to another small village three miles further, called La Riccia, where we found in the *café* three Scotchmen and an Irishman taking refreshments, and speaking English, amongst a lot of Germans, Frenchmen, Italians, and Russians, all chattering their own language, or joining in general conversation in Italian, smoking, and singing, and laughing,—all uniting in the chorus like true citizens of the world. What may be still more curious—all were artists, some in the most grotesque dress, and with curious figure and face. The Frenchman, with his cigar, gay, light, and lively, was humming a French air, and speaking a little French, a little Italian, a little German, or a little English, —all with the greatest *nonchalance* and grace imaginable. The German, with his beard, his long matted hair, his great straw hat, his ornamented pipe, the comfort of his life, and his bundle of linen, had his sketch-book hanging over his shoulder at one side, and his leathern bottle with wine on the other. His long umbrella for the sun, his portable seat under his arm, his walking-stick, and his coarse fustian dress, complete the sketch of this Teutonic artist, as he travelled over the mountains of Italy in search of scenery and subjects of costume.

From this village we went to another called Gensano, about two miles, to see a procession of monks and friars, with their pictures, their candles, and their crosses, &c. &c.—all marching to a band of music, attended by soldiers with their firelocks. The road to this village was crowded with peasants on foot or on mules, the women sitting astride like the men. There were dukes, princesses, and ladies in carriages; and on entering the place we found a very beautiful and very gay scene indeed. There are two streets that run up the side of a hill from one point. Festoons were hanging from bushes, from post to post, all the way up, forming a pleasing barrier to prevent the people from going into the middle of the streets, which were completely carpeted with flowers of all kinds and colours. Opposite each house there was some device of the arms or motto of the family, arranged in compartments in beautiful figures; and at the end of the streets were madonnas hung round with crimson damask, festoons of flowers, and lighted candles. Each window had a piece of silk damask of some bright colour hanging about five or six feet down the wall, upon which the ladies and gentlemen rested their arms. These, with the ladies in gay dresses, the flowers below, the crowds of people in the streets, and the procession with music, produced, I assure you, a delightful and most picturesque effect. Indeed, every year crowds come from Rome, and vehicles of every description are engaged for this day. There were the Duke of Hamilton, with Lord Douglas, his son and his daughter; the Duchess B——, and the Duchess of L—— and her two beautiful daughters; the French ambassador, and the ambassador for the Low Countries, and many other fashionables. The whole ceremony was concluded by a display of fireworks.

When I returned to Albano to bed, I slept soundly; but having smelt the serpents very strong in the woods in the day-time, I still fancied them near me. I rose early next morning, and having hired asses and a guide, my friend and I set off to go up a high mountain, where there is a small monastery and an extensive view. For the greater part of the way the road is a mere path for one person, and so thickly covered by underwood that I was frequently obliged to lie down on the ass's shoulders, to prevent the branches that crossed the road from injuring my eyes. At many parts of the way we crossed a very ancient road, composed of very large stones. On arriving at the top we found about twenty German students, with their asses, their large straw hats, and drawing materials, all as happy, and brotherly, and social as if they were one family. We found also some Scotch people, who, after being accommodated with wine, &c., were making a wretched parley whether they should give the monks twopence-halfpenny each, or fivepence, and could not agree about it; some finally giving the first, and some the latter.

The view from this monastery is most extensive and interesting. In front, and about twenty miles off, lay Rome, as clear and sparkling in the sun as if it were only a mile distant. The atmosphere here is so clear that you can see a house at a distance of thirty or fifty miles, or more. Then we had two or three lakes at our feet, which were sleeping, as it were, in the old craters of burning mountains, the sides of which we had ascended for miles upon the devastating lava, marking by its sinuous appearance the direction it had taken. Between these lakes and Rome lay the Campagna, sterile, flat, and melancholy, with the sea in the distance, and Hannibal's camp on the right — a most beautiful spot for a camp, as it commanded a complete view of that of the Romans, while it was itself scarcely perceptible by them. We returned by another road, if road it might be called, through a wood of chestnut-trees; calling at a monastery to see some very fine pictures by Domenichino. I made our guide drink up the wine, and then trotted him home in high good-humour, singing love-songs in Italian.

Ever yours truly,
W. BEWICK.

Mr. Bewick did not escape the effect of the hot season in Rome, which is generally so trying to the constitution of those who come from more northern and temperate climates. He was reduced to such a state of debility that he found it impossible to continue his labours As a remedy for the oppression from which his whole frame suffered, he was recommended to have recourse to the baths of Nocera. He wisely followed the advice given him, and after passing some months there, found himself so much benefited that he returned to Rome in a comparatively good state of health. The account of his residence there, and of one or two excursions to scenes in the neighbourhood, is very interesting.

Rome, Sept. 10th, 1827.

My dearest Bess,— I returned here on Saturday from the baths of Nocera, whither I was obliged to go in consequence of extreme exhaustion from the hot weather, that oppressed and debilitated my whole frame. Thank God I am now quite well, and as it has begun to rain here I have no fear of further annoyance of this kind, and I am fortunate enough not to have been affected by fever, as is frequently the lot of newcomers to Rome, some of whom suffer severely. The climate at Nocera (upon the crest of the Apennines) is like that in the Highlands of Scotland, and in some other respects the place resembles that country. The people, however, differ widely, the poor peasantry of Italy appearing the most patient and the happiest people on earth; and had you seen the many instances of unalloyed felicity and innocent mirth that were presented to my observation in these mountains, you would be persuaded that true happiness does not depend on wealth, rank, or fashion, as it is often thought to do.

The society at the baths was very circumscribed, and I passed my time in retirement and quiet. The accommodations for visitors are two palazzi, and the bathers I found to be all Italians. One old gentleman spoke a little English, but it was twenty years since he had been in England, so that he had forgotten nearly all. We occasionally had the peasants to dance and sing, to the accompaniment of the guitar and tambourine; and one evening the Marquis Azzoline gave an entertainment upon the top of the mountain, where there was a farm-house.

All the ladies rode on asses, each attended by three men. The whole cavalcade, lighted by torches, ascended the mountains by a narrow and somewhat difficult road. High up we saw our destination, which was brilliantly lighted by lamps and torches, and appeared like an illumination. The Marquis sent me a very spirited, beautiful horse, at which the ladies were not at all pleased, as the narrow path seemed too bounded for his proud spirit; and after conducting them to a safe road, I galloped forward to announce our arrival, when I was received with loud huzzas by about a hundred peasants and the Marquis. The whole scene was splendid. The situation was upon the top of a high mountain surrounded by other mountains; all of which had large fires of wood lighted for the occasion. The farm-house was decorated with lamps, and on the green was a large table covered with the most delicious fruits and wines. This table was surrounded by and canopied with festoons of flowers and box-wood, interspersed with lamps; and adjoining the table was a semicircle enclosed and lighted for music. The dancers were composed of all the neighbouring peasants; the girls dressed in white, with crowns of flowers on their heads.

At the head of the table sat the Duchess of Lante; and (being a foreigner) your humble servant was placed at the right of her Excellency. At the bottom of the table was the Marquis, with the beautiful Princess Donna Giacinta, and her sister Princess Donna Mariamia. The rest of the table was occupied by a countess and her daughter, a governor, and other notables. After the flowers were removed, the servants brought in all manner of eatables, boiled, roasted, fried, baked, and stewed, with wines, champagne, burgundy, malaga, cyprus, &c. The music played, and the girls danced. A poet recited verses, and songs were sung by the peasantry. After midnight the procession began to move again with torches and merriment, when it commenced to rain in torrents, while it thundered and lightened terribly. The ladies screamed, and some fainted, and thus we arrived at our homes wet and weary.

The heat rash that covered my body is quite gone, and I feel quite strong and healthy, and ready to go to work again. On my way here I stopped a day at Terni to see the fall of water, which astonished me. I think I never saw anything so terribly grand, so sublime, so picturesque. The falls of Clyde in Scotland and the Tees, and the fall at Tivoli, are not to be compared with it; indeed, this cascade is thought one of the most beautiful in Europe. The noise of the waterfall may be heard at a great distance, the first fall being three hundred feet in height. The waters fall on the rocks with so much impetuosity that a great part, being reduced almost to vapour, reascends almost to the top of the cascade, where the rays of the sun produce a beautiful rainbow upon the foaming spray. The remainder forms a second fall, and afterwards a third, and lastly uniting with another small river, these waters roll in foaming billows, with thundering noise, along the deep valley.

In the gardens adjoining this fall is a beautiful villa, where our late Queen Caroline lived a short time, and where she received her friends. The fruit in this garden is delicious. After seeing the beauties of the place we returned to the villa, and ate a lunch of figs, pears, apricots, bread and wine, for which we were all prepared, having walked and toiled up the hills and rocks, some on foot, some on asses, and some on chairs carried by men; all Italians but myself. There came some English parties whilst we were enjoying the infinite beauties of the scenery, but they neither seemed to enter into our pleasure, nor receive any pleasurable impression themselves; but were stupidly reserved, and walked about like so many mutes, saying nothing, but looking and going away again in decent and speechless quiet. I went to see the lake of Terni, but was disappointed. The day was not fine, nor was the scenery so beautiful as I expected. I have received a letter from Sir Thomas Lawrence, with a remittance which will serve me for some time. Have you been to Croft or Middleton much? I hope the Rev. J. Dalton and his amiable family are quite well. What is the news at Darlington? How are dear mother and father, and all my sisters? How are Mr. Botcherby, Mr. Janson, Mr. Mewburn, and Dr. Hodgson, and all friends? Sir Thomas Lawrence has written me a very kind and flattering letter.

Yours very sincerely,
W. BEWICK.

CHAPTER IV.

ROME — ENGLISH RESIDENTS IN ROME — EX-QUEEN OF WESTPHALIA — VISIT TO NAPLES — IMPRESSIONS OF THE CITY — NEAPOLITANS FINE DANCERS, BUT REMARKABLY UGLY — DEPRESSING EFFECT OF MOUNT VESUVIUS — ASCENT OF THE MOUNTAIN — POMPEII AND HERCULANEUM — PURCHASE OF ORIGINAL DRAWINGS OF THE OLD MASTERS FOR SIR THOMAS LAWRENCE — SIR THOMAS'S DELIGHT WITH THE 'SIBYL' — FURTHER COMMISSIONS.

MR. BEWICK had now been considerably more than a year in Rome, but every day seemed to add to the weariness of his residence in it. He must have been suffering from the *mal du pays*, for his time was fully occupied; and while he was thus constantly engaged in artistic work, his leisure hours were devoted to the pleasures of society. He was well received in several houses of distinction; his talents were recognised by his brother-artists, and he had the happiness of making the acquaintance of several persons of high station and considerable reputation, in some cases even securing their warm friendship and regard.

In the letter which follows he gives in a few words some discriminating characteristics of the French, German, and English students, and of the manner in which, in their different ways, they derived enjoyment and benefit from their residence in that city which they all regarded as the metropolis of art. In the palaces to which he was invited as a guest, he had opportunities of seeing and studying the *chefs-d'œuvre* of Italian genius; and of these he availed himself, not only to imbue his mind with the highest principles of art, but to learn, so far as he could, those manual secrets of the early painters on which so much of their success as artists depended. It is pleasant to read, in the midst of all the gaieties in which he took part, and the absorption of his mind by the magnificent examples of art to which he had access, of the deep interest which he invariably took in the affairs of his family at home, in all that had reference to the prospects of his brothers, and in all that concerned that sister who appears to have been his principal correspondent. Whatever might occupy his attention at Rome, the burden of his postscripts almost invariably was,

Write soon, with all the news of home. He had also more than one patron in the north of England; as, for instance, Lady Westmorland, to whom reference has already been made, and Mr. Lambton, afterwards Earl of Durham.

Rome, January 1st, 1828.

My dearest Bess,—I wish you all a happy new-year at Darlington. Rome is as dull and stupid as can be. Nothing but religious services, processions and mummery, to break the monotonous quiet of the immortal city. If it were not for the English who come here in the winter, the parties they give, and the bustle they make with their money and their equipages, Rome to an Englishman would be insupportable as a residence, and wearisome as a sojourn, recollecting, as every Englishman must, the comforts of his own country, and the conveniences and gaiety of London. To a student, Rome becomes irksome, unless he can wear away the long nights in the company of some choice friends, very difficult to be met with here, where people only come and go, and you have hardly said 'how do you do' when you are called upon to say, 'good-bye.' The students who have lived here some time get used to the sort of life, and become indifferent and unsocial, many of them living like friars in a convent. I speak of the English; the French and Germans, and students from other countries, I confess are different. They live in a social, Christian-like way, and smoke, and sing, and laugh together; careless, joyous, and happy. The only home an English student has is his studio, a comfortless room, with one window; the walls being coloured grey with soot and whiting, and as dirty as a workshop, with a cold brick-floor, no better than our stables. His bed-room is without fire, without curtains, without carpet, so that he is driven to a *café* in the evening, if he has no invitation to a rout or party. Imagine the discomfort of returning home in silk stockings and thin shoes, at one or two o'clock in the morning, to a lodging without fire, without candle (and perhaps without supper), for the Italians give no refreshment but ice and pastry at their parties. Now this is tiresome if you are young and have an appetite.

This winter I have been out almost every

evening at some party or other. The balls have been very gay, — stars, garters, and orders everywhere. That which I most enjoyed was one at the Neapolitan ambassador's in the Farnese Palace. Imagine this ancient and splendid palace surrounded by torches, and guards, and carriages; the noise and bustle of the servants and soldiers quite astounding. The carriage drives under an immense arched gateway, and we are set down at the bottom of a white marble staircase, wide enough to admit a mail-coach. We ascend, our name is shouted from one livery servant to another, until it reaches the top of the staircase, where stands the padrone or master of the house. To him we make our way through crowds of elegant, fashionable, and beautiful ladies, pay our complinents, and try to see all we can, going from one apartment to another, or dancing. The interiors of the palaces here are magnificent. The saloon of the Farnese palace, of which I am speaking, has the ceiling painted by Carracci most beautifully, and is one of the finest things in Rome as a work of art.

The next ball was given by the Prince and

Princess Doria at their palace. The Dorias are a most ancient Italian family, and their palace is like a little town, splendid in every detail. The picture-gallery was thrown open, and dancing was very spiritedly kept up in it till two o'clock in the morning. The next and most beautiful ball was given by Lady Westmoreland, at her palace — Palazzo Rospilosi. Here there was a profusion of everything; tea, coffee, wine, supper, and every luxury. A very beautiful ball was given by Prince and Princess Lancelotti. The avenues to the palace were all lighted by torches, and the road and walls were covered with a kind of white cloth, and guarded by cavalry. I went with a party of Italians, Neapolitans, and Romans, and the staircase was so crowded with servants that we could scarcely make our way up, and those who announced our names were hoarse with bawling. After about an hour we found the Princess, and I was presented to her. The ball-room was beautiful, the walls and ceiling painted in fresco; but the ices and lemonade were very scarce.

The French ambassador gave a beautiful ball; and several smaller balls were given by

English people of rank and fashion. Lady Drummond and Lady Eyre had each a very nice and select party, and I was introduced to Lady Sandwich, who also gives a ball. There is likewise a charming party every Wednesday at the house of the widow of Lucien Bonaparte, late King of Westphalia, a most elegant and accomplished lady. Her son is with her, Prince Bonaparte, a young man about twenty, who speaks a little English, and is very clever. Lady Westmoreland has given very few *tableaux* this winter. Mr. Lambton is in Paris, he wrote to me from that city. I have also heard from Mr. Bandinel, of the Foreign Office, London, who writes very pleasantly and kindly. I am very glad to hear of Robert, but I have not heard from him. Pray give my kindest remembrance to all. How does Jane go on? and Mary and Tom, and father and mother? I am sadly interrupted just now by the ceremonies at the Sistine Chapel. I am obliged to leave off five days before the ceremony takes place. The young Prince Bonaparte is a splendid horseman, leaping on and off the horse when going at full speed; and he repeated this feat several times when the horses were racing at the Carnival. He is rather short and slim, with a very smart figure, dances elegantly, is fond of speaking English, and often talks with me of horses and politics. The only thing that makes Rome gay just now is the English, who are wintering here, and they appear with their wealth like sovereigns of the world. Mr. Bandinel tells me that business in England is very low. Adieu.

Direct to me at Freeborn, Smith, and Co., Rome. Write soon, and send all news.

His important labours at the Sistine Chapel were often interrupted by a strange cause which prevented him making such progress as he otherwise would. The Pope had an insuperable aversion to the smell of paint, and every time that the sacred edifice was to be the scene of religious ceremonies, Mr. Bewick had to discontinue his labours some days beforehand, and for the time to remove his scaffolding. The constant removal and re-erection of so large a structure entailed a great loss of time, and subjected him to great and frequent annoyance; and it was only that spirit of perseverance which formed so marked a peculiarity in his character which enabled him to carry on to its accomplishment the great work which he had successfully commenced.

Rome, Feb. 28th, 1828.

My dearest Bess,—I have expected to hear from you for some time, and I am anxious to know the reason of your not writing, fearing that you are ill, or that something particular has happened. Pray write immediately, for yours are the only letters I receive here that are at all interesting to me. My brothers never write to me, and as I do not write to any other friends, on account of the expense, it is seldom that I can hear anything in the way of news. Mr. Lambton has sent me a draft for fifty pounds. He signs his letter 'Durham,' according to the title he has just been honoured with; and I suppose I must now speak of him as the 'Earl of Durham.' His influence, of course, will be very much increased, and I should like you to write to Mr. Wilson, to ask him if I am entitled to give a vote for the property at Sunderland, as I certainly should wish to do all I can in return for his attentions and assistance. You need not mention the reason of your asking, because I think Mr. Wilson's friends are of the other party.

In the summer I purpose going to see Naples, Mount Vesuvius, and the interesting country around Naples. The Carnival is over, and was something similar to the last, only I think not so gay or brilliant, which I explain by the fact that nearly all the visitors here are Scotch, and they seldom or never enjoy a thing of this kind. I have not enjoyed it myself so much as last year, and I feel very glad that I entered into the fun so completely as I did the first year. It was truly an enjoyment to me; every one seemed so happy and joyous, and for myself I had just recovered from the rheumatism, and was like one let out of prison. This year, thank God, I have been more careful of the weather—of wet and cold.

I have not been able to go all the winter to the Sistine Chapel, on account of religious ceremonies. The Pope is so particular about the smell of paint or varnish, that I am obliged to leave the chapel, and clear everything out four or five days before His Holiness enters it. I am now once more at work at the Chapel, and I hope in a short time to be able to send something to London. It is curious that Robert has not written to me. When you write, pray tell me all about the family, and write a very long letter. Is Tom in Newcastle still, and John? How is Jane, and how does Anne like London? Mary you must kiss for me! She is my favourite. Tell me how the people at Darlington go on—Mr. Botcherby, Dr. Hodgson, Mr. Mewburn, the solicitor. I hope he is well, and in full practice. You say nothing more of the purchase of the garden ground from Lord Darlington; if you would like to have it, pray buy it.

Rome this winter has been very gay with parties and balls; but parties and balls cost very little here, as there is nothing but ices and lemonade given. Two beautiful entertainments have been given since I wrote to you —one by Lady Crawford, and the other by a Mrs. Starke, a lady who has written a very good guide to Italy—perhaps the best. She likewise gave *tableaux*, that were splendid and quite perfect—one with twenty-eight figures. The ball was attended by masques, and some very good ones; both gave splendid suppers. I have not yet become reconciled to Rome, and I long to see Naples, its beautiful country and antiquities. You may depend upon my writing you everything I meet with worthy of notice. Does my father still read the geography? and my mother—pray tell me how they both are. Everybody here smokes tobacco, or snuffs, or smokes cigars, just as at Darlington.

The weather has been most favourable, and it is more like spring than winter. I do not recollect if I told you that I was introduced to Mr. Ellison, member for Newcastle. He has now left Rome—not in very good health—with his family. I will write to Tom from Naples, to tell him what there is new. I have lost Robert's address. If you will send it to me again, I will write to him, notwithstanding his silence, and to Anne the first opportunity. When you write to Sunderland, pray remember me to all friends, and particularly to Mr. Wilson. I see nobody here from Sunderland; in fact, they are principally Scotch people who are here this year. You tell me nothing of your health. What kind of winter have you had? I suppose as stupid as ever. Desiring you to write me a very long letter,

Believe me, dear,

Ever yours affectionately,

W. BEWICK.

From this period until the month of July we have no other indication of Mr. Bewick's life at Rome. We may infer, therefore, that there was little in it calling for particular notice, and that he was pursuing his usual laborious course, varied only by the gaieties in which he occasionally mingled. The letter which he writes from Naples to his sister manifests great delight in the life and animation of its streets, compared with the apathy of Rome, which he considered a *ville morte*.

Naples, July 12th, 1828.

MY DEAR BESS,—I write this letter looking upon the most beautiful sight perhaps in the world—the Bay of Naples, with a climate the most brilliant and serene. The balmy air fresh from the sea makes it a delightfully healthy situation; and although I have only been here a day or two, I feel invigorated, and in better spirits than at Rome, where the heat was great, and the air oppressive, foggy, and unwholesome. The whole town wore an aspect of lassitude, increased by the multitude of priests and friars, clad in every shade of melancholy colour. Rome is at best a dead place, and in the summer it is deserted for very good reasons. Here at Naples everything is bustle, night and day; and the crowded streets, the shops, the noise, put me in mind of London. Here it may be said that the people 'live;' at Rome they seem only to 'kill time.' Here the soldiers, the bands of music, the drums, the trumpets, the pleasure-boats sailing in the bay, the carriages rattling in the streets, the gaiety of the natives, give an air of life and prosperity to the place, although the people complain very much of poverty and of the want of commerce. The King, the Queen, and the Royal Family, with the Court, drive out every day in carriages with beautiful horses. The soldiers are all drawn out, the trumpets sound, the carriages stop, and everybody takes off his hat as they pass.

The birth-day of the Queen was kept on Sunday with great gaiety. The ships in the bay had all their flags and colours spread, the guns fired, and there was an illumination in the evening. The theatre of St. Carlo—one of the most beautiful I ever saw—was crowded. The seats in the pit are all cushioned, and filled by the most respectable persons; indeed officers of the army and navy are ordered into the pit.

Card-playing seems to be the amusement of the fashionable people here at parties. I was at a party last night, and counted ten tables. No refreshments are given; even at balls a glass of water is all that is asked for, and all that is offered. I have been at two balls, and found nothing else. The people dance very well, but are the ugliest set of men and women I ever saw. Their teeth, owing to the air, are all decayed, and their complexions are very dark. Although the Neapolitans are remarkable for being the gayest and merriest of the Italians, and have most wit, yet I have observed a general dulness and melancholy in the expression of their countenances, particularly if you talk of Mount Vesuvius, when they drop their heads, and speak of it with sorrow; as if it had been sent by the Creator to punish them for being the greatest cheats in the world, which I believe to be the fact, even in the presence of the burning sulphur, and everything that may strike terror by its appearance, or horror by its consequences. Though the mountain is always smoking, and belching forth its fires before their eyes, and raining its fiery showers almost upon their heads, the Neapolitans are still the greatest rogues upon earth, and the veriest cutthroats.

Mount Vesuvius is smoking before me, making the only clouds that are seen in this sky. In the evening the top of the crater within looks red and fiery, and as if it would send forth its bowels of burning stones and molten fire. I think an eruption must be as terrible to witness as its effects are generally dreadful. The eruption this year was very insignificant, and only lasted a few hours. I heard of a man that either fell or threw himself into this caldron three months ago. This person, a shoe-maker of Sorrento, is still living. He was discovered by an Englishman, who, as he was going to the top at the edge of the crater, heard the groans of somebody below;

and looking earnestly down perceived this poor fellow on a ledge of lava below him, with his leg broken. He had lain in this situation for two days, and the only thing he speaks of is a perpetual flitting of fire before his eyes, and an immense cave of fire and red smoke. Should I go to Sorrento I will endeavour to see this man.

The country all about here is sulphurous, everything smacking of it. I drink sulphur-water in the morning and evening, exactly like that of Middleton Spa, but stronger. The wines and fruit are all said to be of a sulphurous nature, and it is dangerous to take much of them. The water is generally bad. The road from Rome, at least half-way near Naples, is not very good to travel in at night, and I think I never saw such cut-throat places. I could give you some melancholy descriptions, but I need not now. I am safe in Naples. By day there is no fear, and by night the roads are well guarded; but still by night I would not risk travelling. I was fortunate enough to have a seat in a gentleman's carriage free of expense, and travelling at suitable times. I have written two letters to Darlington without receiving an answer, one to yourself, and one to Jane; and I have waited some time expecting an answer from one or both. I have written also to Robert, but have no answer yet. Tom sent me a long letter at last, a large sheet. I have sent two pictures to London to Sir Thomas Lawrence. When I have finished the one for Lambton, I hope to be in readiness to return to you all at Darlington, and then what strange stories I shall have to tell you.

I have been very ill with the rheumatism that I caught near Rome, sketching in a damp situation without a seat. It cost me six weeks of terrible pain, but thank God I am now quite well, excepting that I am a little feeble; but with this fresh and healthy air I hope to return to Rome quite stout to finish my work. You speak to me about a guitar. Naples is famous for making these instruments, and I will endeavour to send you one; they are of four strings, and are very elegant. Jane, I hear, is going on in the old way. Mary is very much improved in every respect. Anne still remains in London, which I am glad of. You will be good enough to give my kindest love and remembrance to my father and mother, and all brothers and sisters.

To my friends at Darlington you will be good enough to give my kindest remembrance, and to those at Sunderland. At Naples, goods of every description are bought of English shop-keepers, and I have met in company several Italian gentlemen who speak English very well. The carriage I came to Naples in had the maker's name, G. Marks, New Road, London, at which I laughed heartily, not forgetting my old friend the painter of so many Mount Vesuvius's without ever having seen one eruption. Yesterday I saw a most beautiful villa, built in the most enchanting situation, overlooking the town and bay of Naples; every thing of the newest fashion with fine prints of Lord Darlington's fox-hounds, Mr. Lambton's, and one of King George III. reviewing troops, by Sir Wm. Beechey. In the house where I live the furniture is principally English; the best of it at least. Indeed so many English people come here that I do not wonder at the mania. They pay well, and are imposed upon into the bargain, because they give themselves many airs.

Believe me yours affectionately,

W. Bewick.

Direct to me at Messrs. Cotterell and Co., 10 Largo Della Vittoria, Naples.

Mr. Bewick remained some time in Naples, being much pleased by the new phases of life which that lively city presented to him. He made several excursions to places of interest in and near the city, dared the perils which fifty years ago attended the ascent of Vesuvius, and looked down into its crater. Herculaneum and Pompeii had not been so thoroughly exposed to the light of day as they now are, but what was visible of them he examined with the interest of one who saw in antiquities much that might be rendered subservient to his art. While at Naples he not only received a highly appreciatory letter from Sir Thomas Lawrence, but was commissioned by him to look out for original drawings by the old masters—a task in which he anticipated little success, as the French had been engaged in the same search before him, and had collected almost everything that was worthy of removal.

Naples, Sept. 4th, 1828.

MY DEAR BESS,—Your very obliging letter I received gladly, and am very happy to hear you are all well at home. I have likewise heard from Robert, who is in good health, but anxious to pass the examination in London; and as his time will be at an end with his present master very soon, he is anxious to go to London and attend lectures immediately after leaving Boxford.

Since writing to you I have been up to the top of Mount Vesuvius, and I will recount to you at Darlington my journey, and what kind of thing it is. The company I went with were fifteen in number, with seven men-servants and a lady's-maid, and consisted of a Roman princess and two daughters, Mr. and Miss Brown, nephew and niece, and Lady Lubbock, two cavaliers, officers of the King's body-guard, two sons of a noble Neapolitan, one of the King's couriers, a Roman councillor, your humble servant, and a gentleman who undertook to be our director, and who had made the same excursion in company with Mrs. Starke (who has published her travels). The company left Naples at half-past nine in the evening, in three carriages, and arrived at the little village of Resina at eleven, the full moon swimming in the cloudless sky. We drove into the yard of the captain of the guides, named Salvatone Madonna, which was filled with asses, mules, and men, all ready to set off for the mountain. The entrance of the carriages, the uproar and eagerness of the men to obtain riders, caused a noise and confusion that was as astounding and as laughable as a Neapolitan rabble could be expected to make.

From this place we were taken to a *tratorica*, half a mile distant, by the side of the sea, where was prepared a supper that was as useless as it was tormenting, every one wishing to proceed, and no one having any appetite, for we were all anxious to be upon the verge of the crater before sunrise. However, the maccaroni was upon the table, and I partook heartily of fish and champagne, and mounted my donkey in the crowd below, with eager anticipations of what was to come—of hair-breadth escapes by flood and field, of robbers, assassins, and of all that fiction, history, the experience of the past, and the facts of the present, could suggest to my imagination.

The roads here are all of lava, and you travel on the accumulation of ages, the guide giving you an account of the different strata. Thus we journeyed on, passing through rich vineyards, the watch-dogs barking and giving notice of our passing, and the peasants running to the road to see that all was right with the fruit. We arrived by crooked and unpleasant paths at the Hermitage, a small white house with a chapel, a hermit, and a guard of six or seven soldiers, stationed there for the benefit of Vesuvian travellers. This guard has been placed there since the robbery of some French gentlemen, at the foot of the cone of the mountain, a short time ago. Some of the banditti have been taken and sent to the galleys, and there remain still four or five who have eluded the vigilant search of the guard. These robbers have property near the village. The story was told to me by my guide, whose brother happened to be guide to these same Frenchmen, as we rode past the spot. He was forced with his face to the ground, and a musket at his head to confess who the travellers were, one of them having a star at his breast. The story, told by moonlight upon the very spot, made me look apprehensively around, the situation being a very dreary one, and by night or day admirably calculated for any black or bloody deed, for it looked on all sides a desert formed of masses of lava, black as pitch, sinking into cavities, holes, curious corners, dells, and dry river-beds made by descending torrents.

We passed this part of the road in comparative stillness, for every one had enough to do to look to his ass; and the path, which is as bad as it can well be, seemed as if made for difficulty and danger. We had tea, with roast beef, and fowls, and a little brandy, at the Hermitage, and then we mounted our asses, and rode on, accompanied by two or three of the soldiers, to the foot of the cone of the mountain, where, dismounting and taking large sticks, we prepared to ascend; the ladies being placed in arm-chairs fixed on poles, and carried by six or eight men. The difficulty and danger were really so great that I wonder, when I reflect on it, that no accident happened. Never was such a scene, with tugging and tumbling, the rolling of stones from above, the screams of women, the shouting, bawling and swearing of men — who, instead of invoking the Madonna, or some goodly saint, called upon the aid of maccaroni,—the laughing of some, and the lamentation of others. The curious and novel appearance of the party from below, seen stretching from the bottom to the top in picturesque and terrible positions, was very remarkable. Some seemed falling from fatigue, and others were lying on the mountain taking breath, while the men encouraged each other to exertion, —the leader of the guides, dressed in white, standing apart, exhorting his subordinates, while the soldiers with their muskets ran up to the top to see that all was right there, and that there were no lurkers. All together formed a scene as picturesque and romantic as it was dangerous, and often ridiculous.

When we were nearly at the top the sun began to rise, lighting up splendidly the most extensive as well as the most beautiful scenery that fancy could conjure up. The Bay of Naples spread out below, like an immense mirror, the surface studded with fishing-boats with white sails, while the breath of morning slightly rippled the blue water. The city lay circling the extensive margin of this delicious crescent with its cold white houses, and numerous towns and villages seemed to be melting into air in the distance.

A few more steps brought us to the verge of the crater of Vesuvius, and a more awful or sublime sight it is impossible to conceive. The first impression was one of awe and terror. Pictures or descriptions can give but a very faint idea of the grandeur of this immense amphitheatre, smoking, rumbling, and belching forth with hideous noise. its crimson tongues of fire, the earth trembling under you, and menacing every instant an explosion that might scatter your limbs piecemeal over the scene so far below. A convulsion of nature like this is a curious and very interesting sight, and never fails to impress upon the beholder the omnipotence of the Creator.

The top of the cone of this mountain is said to be about three and a half miles in circumference—it looks about a mile. The inside of the crater is an immense cavern, black with fire and smoke; and in the centre rises another cone formed of black lava, from the top or point of which issue constantly volumes of smoke, rising majestically into clouds above, or enveloping the summit; and every two or three minutes burst forth with thundering noise a column of fire of red-hot lava, hissing and spitting. The noise may be said to resemble the bellowing of some gigantic wild beast chained below, and the loud thunderous rumbling may be likened to the clanking of his chains. Think, then, what must be the effect of an eruption that devastates the country around!

Well may the Neapolitans look melancholy and hang their heads when you talk of Vesuvius. It is said that an eruption in 472 was so terrible that the inhabitants of Constantinople were terrified; and in another, the clouds of stones and ashes thrown out darkened the sun at Rome, and even some stones were carried by the wind as far as Egypt. That stones from this mountain have been found two hundred miles distant is certain, but that they could be hurled as far as Egypt is hard to believe. The descent to the point where we left the asses and mules was as rapid as the ascent was slow, and took one hour, three minutes, every step carrying you three or four yards down knee-deep in pumice-stone, ashes, and scoria. If instead of putting your heel down first, you were to put your toe, you would fall, and death would be inevitable, such is the fatal facility of the descent.

My kindest and dearest remembrance to all my family, and believe me truly and affectionately yours,

W. BEWICK.

From Naples, Sept. 5th, 1828.

Naples, Nov. 11th, 1828.

MY DEAREST BESS,—Your very obliging and excellent letter, dated so long ago as September 17th, I have this day received, and I derive much consolation, not only from the expressions, but from the manner in which the whole is written. It gives me great pleasure that Tom is again well, and gone to his occupation, and that all the other members of the family are in good health and spirits; particularly my dear father and mother. You never say if Anne and her husband are still in London. The plants Jane wishes me to bring I hope are for her own garden, and the silk-worms for mother will be for the mulberry-trees that are yet to be planted. I am delighted with your opinion of John. Dear Mary, too, is merry and laughing as usual. Happy girl! I hope she will choose a husband who will deserve her, for she was always my favourite, and her sisters can allow me to say as much without jealousy.

Naples is filling with English people, and it is becoming rather cold. The grapes are all finished, and the vineyards are all being dressed for next year. New wine is brought on the table; pears, apples, grapes, and roasted chestnuts form the dessert; and this dessert, which would cost half-a-crown or three shillings in England, will cost for one person three half-pence or two-pence. The grapes are most exquisite, as well as the peas and apples. There is a fruit I like very much called the white water-melon, gushing with the most delicious juice. The orange-trees are bending with their golden fruit, and the lemons are ready for the punch. You buy an orange nearly as large as your head for a farthing or halfpenny. The pomegranates, too, are bursting with ripeness, showing their rich, ruby insides, more tempting in appearance than in taste. The climate here, although a little cold in the morning, is like the spring in England. The people sit with their windows open all day long, and sup in the street by moonlight at night, singing and playing the guitar; and it is a curious fact that, amidst wine and merriment, you never see any one tipsy or behaving rudely.

Since writing the above I have received a most pleasant letter from Sir Thomas Lawrence, who informs me that the pictures I sent to him have arrived in the river, and that, as soon as they come to his house, he will show them to his brother Academicians, and write me faithfully the impression they make. The letter is excessively gratifying, and if the expense was not so much I should be tempted to send it to you to read. I am just recovering from a cold in my head and throat, that I think I got upon the high mountains near this city, and I have been tempted to buy some pictures here by the old masters, such as Raphael. What can Mr. Sams be doing in Jerusalem?

Believe me, dearest, yours affectionately,

W. BEWICK.

I have seen Pompeii and Herculaneum, where they are still making excavations, and find every day something curious. The town of Pompeii is a most melancholy and interesting sight. You see the houses, the baths, the pavements, the sacred edifices, and the public halls; the prisons, the stocks, the theatres, the sepulchres, and the monuments of public men or private families; statues, pictures of the highest style of art, and of the very best workmanship; buildings and columns left unfinished; nay, here are their fire-places, with the ashes of the fire; the wine dried up in the bottles; corn, beans, and oats unground, flour ready for bread, and even bread and eggs; figs, olives, almonds, cherries, prunes, linen, cloth, bottles, glasses, cups, spoons, chairs, locks and keys, earrings, necklaces, rings, bracelets, pins, needles, inkstands, and pens—all of the most exquisite taste and invention; frying-pans, girdles, sauce-pans, ladles made of bronze, and lined with silver (tin not being known); lamps and stands, wonderfully beautiful, and vases, hay, ropes; a purse with money found in one hand of a lady, and a key in the other, supposed to be the lady of the house. The skeleton was found with most beautiful gold ornaments, necklace, earrings, and armlets.

When you view the streets, houses, and monuments of Pompeii, and look not only upon specimens of most exquisite art, but also upon the utensils of the kitchen, the materials for eating and drinking, and even the marks of cups and glasses upon marble tables in the drinking-shops, there remains upon the mind an impression of astonishment, for Pompeii was destroyed, or covered entirely, by the ashes of Mount Vesuvius in the year 79 after the birth of Christ. All the articles at Pompeii are not burnt; but those at Herculaneum are burnt black like charcoal; and the pictures brought to light, painted on the walls at Pompeii, are most beautifully preserved, and, what most astonishes me, of the most perfect style of art. Some of them deserve to be classed with the finest specimens of painting of the best periods of modern art.

I am looking out for original drawings by the old masters for Sir Thomas Lawrence; but I am afraid that I shall not be at all successful, as the French have carried away everything that was at all worth taking, and since then so many English have bought and taken away pictures that the gleanings are scarce, and if anything good and genuine is found, it is exorbitantly dear. I drank all your healths on the 20th of October, knowing that you would all be together in the evening. Farewell.

Early in the following year Mr. Bewick's correspondence shows that he was again in Rome, where he was executing some commissions with which he had been favoured. The copies of the pictures in the Sistine Chapel which he had sent home met with the highest approbation of Sir Thomas Lawrence, who had them put up in his rooms.

In a letter to Bewick Sir Thomas says: 'I have sincere apologies to make to you for not sooner informing you of my receipt of the two pictures, which I had immediately placed on substantial frames. Unfortunately their large size makes it difficult for me to exhibit them in the rooms, which, with my own too numerous works, their superior dimensions convert into very small apartments. But let me now speak of the works themselves. I am not disappointed in their grandeur and noble simplicity of effect, but I will own to you that I am not equally satisfied with two or three of the details. In the "Sibyl" my impression is that something has been lost in the expression of the countenance, which my memory tells me has in the original a more softened abstraction of thought in the character. Then in the advancing leg the shadow comes on so far and harshly on the sight that the width, fulness, and substance of the limb, are injured by it.

'Is there so great a distance from the nose to the ear of the "Jeremiah," which by-the-bye is small, and not accurately placed, and have you sufficiently attended to the fine anatomical drawing of the upper hand, the first joint of the forefinger? The knuckle appears rather a large swelling than the form itself, which in Michael Angelo is generally pronounced.

'These are my criticisms, and being anxious for the complete defence of this greatest artist, and its successful effect by your pencil, I have at present abstained from showing the pictures, but shall soon exhibit them to my friends. Of the sale of the "Jeremiah" you may be certain, as should other purchasers not be found, I shall gladly retain it at the price I sent you for the other.

* * * * * *

'I cannot well undertake the responsibility of employing you on another figure from the same noble work; but should you, without building on my assistance, choose to dedicate your time to it, let me hope that your judgment will coincide with mine in selecting the "Sibyl" half rising and closing the book.'

In reply to this letter and the criticisms which it contains, Mr. Bewick writes :—' I am sorry that the size of the "Jeremiah" and the "Sibyl" prevents you from placing them in apartments where perhaps distance and light properly arranged might be favourable. The space in the chapel where they were painted is, as you know, immense, and the distance of the originals sixty feet from the spectator, with a light rather obscure, which may tend very much to soften any harshness of effect or expression that may have impressed you with a confined distance and concentrated light close upon the pictures.

'In answer to your very obliging criticisms on one or two details that you have been so kind as to make to me, I feel inclined rather to acknowledge the defects for my own than en-

deavour to make a feeble defence at the expense,
if it was possible, of the original author. I confess to you that the expression of the "Sibyl" I
found to be most difficult to hit; and I made
the observation at the time that by approaching
close to the head the individuality in a great
measure lessened that abstraction that distance
and obscurity gave. Whether this may be true
with regard to my copy I will not pretend to
say — no one made the remark when comparing
it with the original in the chapel. I should
have been too happy for a remark of this kind,
for it is a head which I took great trouble to
get well. The advancing leg, which you may
depend upon being exactly copied, always appeared to me to have something of the objection
you mention. The defect of the ear and the
upper hand of "Jeremiah" I should be most glad
to take as my own; they are both very much
defaced in the fresco. The upper hand is not at
all comparable to the one below, hanging, the
veins surcharged, and every articulation beautifully and powerfully pronounced. Perhaps
nothing could be finer than the expression of
this hand, but the other is feeble, flat, and

rather awkwardly drawn—as you say, lumpy. It must have lost much of its original force and character.'

Haydon, it may be remarked, though he admired the manner in which Bewick had accomplished the task which he had undertaken, did not approve of it. 'What absurdity,' he remarked, 'to pull things from dark recesses, sixty feet high—things which were obliged to be painted lighter, drawn fuller, and coloured harder than nature warrants, to look like life at the distance, and to bring them down to the level of the eye in a drawing-room, and adore them as the purest examples of form, colour, expression, and character. They were never meant to be seen at that distance or in that space.'

The following letter is addressed by Bewick to his sister :—

Rome, March 25th, 1829.

DEAREST BESS,—I have waited ever since I wrote to you from Naples, but in vain, neither my brother Robert nor yourself have sent to me an answer, although it is two months since I wrote to both. Since my arrival here I have been working very hard at the small picture for Lord Durham, which I hope to finish soon. The subject is 'Cornelia' and her family, from Roman history. A Roman lady exhibits her jewels to Cornelia, who in reply shows her her two boys; you remember the story. As Lord Durham is the father of a beautiful and interesting family, I thought it would please both himself and Lady Durham. He was satisfied, and I am now going on with the picture, which, I am sorry to say, is but small, but it is according to his orders. Sir Thomas Lawrence has written to me that he has put up the pictures in his room—that he is struck with their 'noble grandeur,' &c., &c., and that the scale being so large his rooms have become small apartments. Sir Thomas says, 'He will be glad to see Robert when he does him the honour to call upon him.' I hope that my brother has already called, as I wrote to him to do so. Sir Thomas tells me not to be uneasy about the sale of the other picture, as if no purchaser appears he will take it himself, and requests me, if I have time, to occupy myself upon another 'Sibyl,' which he names, and likewise desires me, if possible, to make him a facsimile copy of a large original drawing by Michael Angelo, which is in the Museum of Naples.

It is unfortunate that he had not told me before I left Naples, as I could have made a drawing very well when I was there. I am afraid that it will not be possible for me to deny Sir Thomas what he requests, though it will cost me a run over to Naples for a week or two. He has been so remarkably kind to me, as you know, that I think it might be imprudent not to do any little thing I can to please him. I am extremely anxious to hear from you, to know how you are, and still more anxious to be at Darlington, which I hope now will not be long. I work hard every day in this hope, and trust soon to see you all. I wonder and wonder you have not written, and more so at Robert, because his marriage was to take place about this time, and he may well guess how glad I shall be to hear it has taken place. How does Jane's affair come on? Is Thomas gone to London? Pray tell me all news.

On my coming to Rome I met a number

of English travellers and foreigners, who were leaving on account of the death of the Pope. All the theatres were closed, and every amusement was stopped, so that this Eternal City was, if possible, more dull than ever. The defunct sovereign was placed in state in St. Peter's, and a most splendid cenotaph erected to his honour, or his memory, in the centre of the Cathedral. The ceremonial was in the usual pompous style, and might strike an English stranger as a gaudy show for the living rather than sincere tribute of respect to the dead.

The Romans are now in lively suspense for the election of the new pontiff, which must take place shortly. The conclave of Cardinals is sitting, and the only amusement that the people enjoy is to go to Monte Cavallo, before the Royal Palace of the Quirinal, twice a day to see the smoke and inquire the news of the day. The seeing the smoke is this. You must know that twice a day the votes for the new Pope are collected from the Cardinals, and if a sufficient number do not vote for the Cardinal proposed, the votes, which are written on paper, are burnt in a stove, from which there is a pipe to convey the smoke outside, in front of the palace. This, so long as it continues, is a sign that the Pope is not yet elected. When the smoke ceases, the votes are not burnt, and of course no smoke appears. The whole of the Cardinals are locked up for the time, without the slightest communication with any one. Their victuals are conveyed to them every day, as in a nunnery, by a wheel, without their seeing any one. There is a strong guard at the entrance of the palace, and no one enters it or comes out. It is exactly like a prison. Every one has his two apartments and one servant, and thus they live a tiresome and unwholesome life. The whole of the Christian world is waiting anxiously the result of their holy deliberations.

I still find the air of Rome very heavy, and often damp, producing a low tone of nerves, from which arise melancholy and dulness of spirits; and I have no doubt that the air of Naples suits me much better than that of this city, which is so irregular that scarcely two days are at the same temperature, one hot and another cold or damp. Pray write immediately and tell me all news. How are mother and father? Mary?—Jane?—Is John Graham in Darlington, and what is he doing? My journey from Naples was, although a little cold, very pleasant. Pray give my kindest compliments to Mr. Wilson of Sunderland, Dr. Burn, and all friends, and believe me to be,

Yours affectionately, and ever truly,

W. BEWICK.

CHAPTER V.

RETURN TO ENGLAND — HIS LABOURS WARMLY APPROVED BY SIR THOMAS LAWRENCE — ENCOUNTER WITH HIS OLD FRIEND HAZLITT — INTERVIEW WITH NORTHCOTE — HOUSE IN GEORGE STREET, HANOVER SQUARE — ACCOUNT OF BEWICK'S DRAWINGS IN THE ART-UNION — LETTERS TO TWO FRIENDS — REMINISCENCES OF HIS ARTISTIC EDUCATION — ART-LANGUAGE.

It was not without considerable injury to his health, long delicate, that Mr. Bewick had painted his copies of the 'Delphic Sibyl' on a scaffolding sixty feet high, erected by him in the Sistine Chapel, and afterwards of 'Jeremiah lamenting the destruction of Jerusalem;' but the warm approval of the President and of the artists to whom they were exhibited on their arrival in England was a rich reward to him, and he was in high spirits at receiving Sir Thomas's order for copies of the whole series of Prophets and Sibyls. He had executed four large copies in oil, and the whole of the studies in detail, when the sudden death of Sir Thomas Lawrence put a stop to his labours, and induced him to return to England. The Academy did not feel itself called upon to carry out the purpose of its great President, and the four careful and magnificent copies were sold at the sale of Sir Thomas Lawrence's effects, and are hidden away in some corner where they are useless, alike to the student and the connoisseur. A large collection of drawings, however, from which the paintings had been made remained in the artist's hands, and in his declining years it was his happiness to be able to add a gallery to his house in Leskerne, where he could show them with other original drawings and paintings of his own, as well as with some choice specimens of the old masters gathered in his travels. But surely such works are of national interest, and should be placed in some national museum or gallery as pendants to the Cartoons of Raffaelle.

The first record in Bewick's own handwriting of what befell him on his return to England is an account of a final meeting with Hazlitt and an interview with the painter Northcote.

On my return from Italy I met my old friend Hazlitt near Trafalgar Square. When he saw me he rushed up to me and caught me by both hands, exclaiming in amazement, 'My dear fellow, where have you come from? where have you been? I have lost sight of you for an age.' I replied, 'I have been in the sunny clime, and am just on my way to Northcote to show him my "Jeremiah."' 'Ah! I am so glad you are just come as my redeeming star,—my credit is at this time very low with him; you must know I am editing his Fables—I may say writing them—and he is just now very peevish and impatient at my not sending him some "copy." I shall be ready to-morrow. Now if you see him to-day and put him into a good humour, which you will do by showing him your "Jeremiah"— you must speak of me, tell him you have just seen me, and that I shall see him to-morrow with more "copy," and then you can tell me how his pulse beats,' &c.

We then shook hands and parted, he going his way, I to Northcote. An old servant, almost blind, who had lived with him for half-a-century, and who had been ordered to leave scores of times, but would not go, opened the door. I sent in my card, and was ushered into the miser's study. I found him alone in his studio, dressed in an old dingy green dressing-gown, and cap to match. He received me very graciously, and when I told him I had just returned from Italy he opened his eyes with amazement. I said I had brought my drawing of 'Jeremiah' to show him. 'Thank you, thank you, Mr. Bewick,' he said. I then unrolled my drawing; and he, holding up his hands in amazement, said, 'Ah! wonderful — strange! How grand! Ah, sir, Raphael and Michael Angelo were grand fellows —we are puny and meagre compared with them, and I fear ever shall be. The style of education in the arts is so effeminate, if I may so speak, in this country.' Then in a sententious manner he added, 'No, sir, they will never be able to comprehend the grandeur of Michael Angelo; you may show "Jeremiah" upside down for the next century, and no one will see the difference, so unaccustomed are they to see, and so little do they know of the grand lines and bold conceptions of Michael Angelo. Now, there is your friend, Mr. Hazlitt; he is clever, and has a critical conception of art, but he cannot comprehend Michael Angelo. For instance, he tells me respecting the Sistine Chapel, that he was disappointed with the " Last Judgment," that the Prophets and Sibyls are grand figures, but that they are wanting in elevated expression.' ' But,' said I, ' had he been upon the cornice where I was he would have seen the expression better. I do not think that from a distance of sixty feet below he could distinguish their characteristics. He speaks of " Jeremiah" not being so fine in the expression of the features as in the action of the body, and drapery, hands, &c. Now I do not agree with him. The absorbed expression of grief or abandonment to lamentation in the face of " Jeremiah" is as fine and concentrated, as elevated and perfectly worked out, as finished as a miniature, as anything I know of Raphael; and I question if Raphael has ever given such grandeur of conception in any one figure. Then there is the face of the Delphic Sibyl, what can be more inspired, more elevated, poetical, or even beautiful ?' *N*. ' He mentions Zachariah, Daniel, &c.' *B.* ' But then there is Joel, Isaiah, the Cumæan

Sibyl, all equal in characteristic expression, intense, abstract, in unison with the action of the figure—with that grandeur of epic art which Sir Joshua says there is nothing to equal. Mr. Hazlitt has not been near enough to see the individual peculiarities or wonderful artistic excellence of their heads. By-the-bye this conversation reminds me that I have just seen our friend Hazlitt.' *N.* 'You have, have you? He is the strangest being I ever met with; what did he say?' *B.* 'He is ready with fresh "copy," and will see you to-morrow.' At this piece of information Northcote rubbed his hands, and smiling said, 'Well, Hazlitt is a clever, but original genius; I can make nothing of him, but hope he will come—very odd, very odd!' I then rolled up my 'Jeremiah,' bid Northcote good morning, and beset my steps to Mr. Hazlitt, who was anxious to learn my success. I told him the way was all made straight for him, and that Mr. Northcote would be glad to see him. He shook me warmly by the hand, and we parted. I left town for a time, and an occasional correspondence was kept up. But I never shook hands with him again.

On his return to England Mr. Bewick took a house in George Street, Hanover Square, for the purpose of exhibiting his works. They naturally excited much interest in artists, though unhappily for the country they were left on his hands, and not secured for any school of art. The following detailed account of the drawings exhibited by Mr. Bewick, and of the manner in which they were taken, is copied from a contemporary notice in the *Art-Union:*—

'In the year 1826, Sir Thomas Lawrence commissioned Mr. Bewick, then in Rome, to make a series of copies from the most famous works of Michael Angelo—the Prophets and Sibyls that adorn the chapel of the Pontiff. It was the intention of the President to present these copies to the Royal Academy, in order that the future student might be enabled to consult the magnificent creations of a mighty mind, and derive from the continual study of them that incentive to emulation, and that instruction in his art, which these wonderful productions could not fail to afford him. Unfortunately for the artist and the country, the

President died before the labour was completed. Four only of the copies had been made; and these, unhappily, having been disposed of at the sale of his property, are hidden in some corner to which the student is debarred access. A large collection of drawings, however, from which the paintings were to have been made, is still in the possession of Mr. Bewick; and to these we desire to direct public attention, with the hope that we may be the means of consigning them to their original destination.

'When Sir Thomas selected Mr. Bewick for the performance of this arduous duty, he had, no doubt, entire conviction of his fitness for the task; he had the power to choose from the whole range of students; for probably there was not one who would not gladly have undertaken it, as conferring a high and honourable distinction, and as supplying the surest and most effectual mode of professional improvement. The wisdom of the choice is proved by the manner in which the work has been executed. The finished paintings we have not seen; but the drawings are of so admirable a character, that we cannot doubt their preserving the amazing power and beauty of the originals.

'The difficulty of procuring them was by no means small. The influence of Sir Thomas Lawrence overcame the first obstacle; and permission was granted to Mr. Bewick to make the copies. The height of the Sistine Chapel is sixty feet; and the scaffolding was carried up close to the ceiling. This scaffolding, it was necessary frequently to remove and re-erect in consequence of the ceremonials appointed to take place therein. The time required was necessarily very great; and a residence in Rome during the summer months—so perilous to health and life—is what few are disposed to encounter. There are, indeed, many ways of accounting for the fact that of the students resident in, or visiting Rome, none have had the courage, energy, and industry to grapple with difficulties which appeared almost insurmountable, even after the labour had been promised recompense, and permission to undertake it had been obtained. Notwithstanding the strong incentive to exertion supplied by Sir Joshua Reynolds, a few sketches of the great works in the Sistine Chapel have been all that artists have brought away; and neither the French, the Germans, nor the Russians, who throng in crowds to the Eternal City to study the mighty master, have obtained a more advantageous mode of making the world acquainted with his greatness. It is therefore most unlikely that other copies than those of Mr. Bewick will be made; and in duty to him, as well as the students in Great Britain, we express an earnest hope that these may not be scattered, and so lost to the world. The whole of the interior of the Chapel Sixtus is divided into compartments, varied in size and form, all occupied with subjects relating to Holy Writ, or in that sublime circle, exhibiting the origin, the progress, and final dispensations of theocracy, or the empire of Religion, considered as the parent and queen of man, as taught by the sacred records. In this imagery of primeval simplicity, whose sole object is the relation of the race to its founder, there is only God with man. The veil of eternity is rent: time, space, and matter, teem in the creation of the elements and of earth. The awful synod of Prophets and Sibyls are the heralds of the Redeemer; and the host of Patriarchs the pedigree of the Son of Man. Such is the spirit of the Sistine Chapel.

'Among the copies are the five Sibyls—Delphica, Cumæa, Persica, Lybica, and Erythræa. The first is the most wonderful—a combination of beauty with power in the countenance, such as no other painter has ever executed, or, perhaps, ever conceived. The aged Persica pores over a book. Lybica is rising and closing a volume. Of the Prophets, Isaiah is listening to a sacred messenger; Jeremiah is mourning over the fearful nature of his own prophecies; Joel is perusing a scroll; Ezekiel, Zachariah, and Daniel, are the others. But any attempt to describe them would be absurd. The drawings are larger than life-size, and upon a scale of about one half of the originals. They may, we presume, be seen where we have seen them, at the house of Mr. Bewick, No. 27 George Street, Hanover Square.

'It is unnecessary for us to state that in

thus strongly lauding this series of copies by
Mr. Bewick—and in treating them with some
portion of that enthusiasm all artists have felt
in examining, and afterwards remembering, the
originals—we are influenced only by an earnest
desire to assist in securing them, as the property of the country, for the benefit of British
students in art. We look upon them as certain
sources of future greatness to many a young
and yet uninformed mind, and trust there may
be no danger of their being withheld from a
national depository. But as the Chancellor of
the Exchequer may, from a score of causes,
plead the inability of the nation to spare from
its coffers the enormous sum of a few hundred
pounds to bestow them on the country, we hope
the members of the Royal Academy will, if the
Chancellor do not, carry out the design of their
late President, and expend some portion of their
funds upon the most legitimate purpose to which
they can be applied.

'We are naturally anxious to secure them
for the metropolis, where they might be studied
by and teach the greater number; but if any
difficulty should arise to prevent this—and if

any do we shall feel no little sorrow and shame for the apathy of promoters and encouragers of British Art—we still hope they may not be so divided and scattered that, when a more auspicious time arrives, it will be impossible again to gather them together. Some provincial town will, perhaps, possess the treasure, and we may foresee a period when the student will make a pilgrimage to visit them with as much enthusiastic zeal as ever bore a devotee through toil to some sacred shrine.

'Sure we are that if our observations induce artists to look at these glorious works, the creations of the mightiest mind that has existed since human beings ceased to be directly inspired, they will consider us fully borne out in the earnest enthusiasm with which we speak of them.'

Mr. Bewick's health at this time was so delicate that he was unable to visit much at night, but his friends still cherish the recollection of the happy evenings spent in George Street, with him, his wife, and his bright and pretty sister.

But Darlington was his home, and thither he returned, finding large occupation for his ready pencil, for everybody in that part of the world who could afford it considered it his duty to have his portrait painted by 'Bewick,' or to have his walls adorned with some specimen of his handiwork; so that before long the artist was enabled to retire from painting as a profession.

When the Commission was appointed, in 1843, to award prizes for designs of high art calculated for the fresco adornment of the Houses of Parliament, Bewick arose, like a war horse at the sound of the trumpet, and prepared a cartoon, entitled 'The Triumph of David,' which he announced thus in a letter to Sir C. Eastlake :—

Dear Sir,—I have finished a drawing for the forthcoming competition, and as I have no place near Westminster Hall, where I could have a day to sketch it and retouch it privately, in case of accident by friction, or by conveyance from such a distance as this, I write to ask you if any such convenience will be accorded to artists from the country like myself. The very frail material of chalk on such a scale makes it rather an anxious consideration, when it is not fixed by any process of steaming, and I have not attempted to try the experiment with mine. I trust there will be sufficient forethought and provision for the treatment in hanging drawings on this large scale without frames, when the subject fills to the very edge of paper, as mine does; a thumb-mark or rule would be an injury.

I had almost given up the idea of sending a drawing, by reason of the delicate state of my health during the winter, and the promising information given in a former number of the *Art-Union* — 'that the walls will be so crowded,' but as a very contrary expectation is expressed in the *last* number of that publication (that the competition would be only a remove from a failure), I feel stimulated to send you what I can get ready; and although it is not done with the advantages of models, &c., that I might have had in London, I still entertain a humble hope that the 'judges' may not pass my design without discovering traces of some former acknowledged power in this particular department of chalk-drawing.

Sir Charles Eastlake replied courteously to this letter, as he did on all occasions, but as there is nothing in his letter beyond the details of business, it seems hardly worth while to print it.

The cartoon appears to have been rather too delicate in its treatment to excite much attention among the large number of drawings sent in for competition; but in the autumn it was exhibited at Darlington together with the artist's Sistine copies, and attracted much interest.

Henceforth he came forward but little into public life, his easy circumstances at home and the delicacy of his health alike persuading him of the charms of his fireside. The letters written in his declining years to his friends, Mr. W. Davison of Hartlepool and Mr. H. Cromek of Wakefield, show how completely he was devoted to his art, and how he loved to recall the circumstances of his early life, and especially all details connected with his ever-regretted master. While he was in Rome, and intimate with Gibson, the sculptor had made a cast of Bewick's head, which Mrs. Bewick subsequently desired to have executed in marble. With reference to this subject Gibson writes from Rome :—

Rome, March 1st, 1847.

Dear Bewick,—Many thanks for your kind letter and remembrance of me. I hope your health will improve. I continue to enjoy pretty good health, though never very strong—always careful, abstemious, and regular in my habits.

I devote all my soul and body to my art, and rise up with the sun. Since you left Rome I have produced many works in marble and original drawings. My life being so active, months and years gallop over my head with great rapidity. Old age and death will ere long put an end to my labours. My labours will live to be judged of by man, and my soul by God.

The cast of your bust has been preserved. If you wish to have it I can send it to you—executed in marble it will cost you twenty pounds; for such a bust I charge seventy pounds. I think my agent in London, Mr. M'Cracken, Old Jewry, will charge you five pounds for case, packing, and carriage from Rome to London. So your bust, to which I should give myself some finishing touches, would cost you twenty-five pounds put down in London.

I remain, dear Bewick,
Yours very sincerely,
JOHN GIBSON.

The bust was put into marble, but did not reach Haughton-le-Skerne until the August of 1855, and the pleasant excitement produced by its arrival is described in a letter of the period.

Mr. Bewick was now in that happy position in which he could pursue his art, not as a means of living, but for the pleasure it afforded him. In his correspondence with the two intimate friends to whom the following letters were addressed, we see how deep was the artistic feeling by which he was animated, and how anxious he was to obtain to still higher excellence. Ever mindful of the difficulties which he had encountered in the early part of his career, he was at all times eager to encourage struggling artists, always urging them to perseverance as the road to success where there is a foundation of true talent.

As he had been unable to dispose of his large copies of the cartoons, he had rooms prepared for them connected with his own house; but symptoms of mildew soon showed themselves, and he found it necessary to use some necessary precautions in order to preserve them. At the same time, he still executed occasional commissions; his works were becoming known far and wide; and he was even solicited to allow his copies of Michael Angelo's cartoons to be exhibited in New York. These and similar matters are referred to in the following letter to his friends; and this portion of his correspondence is particularly interesting for the insight it gives us into his domestic life, showing his amiable character as a man, his obliging disposition as a friend, and his affectionate character as a husband and father. These letters are valuable also for the occasional reminiscences of artists with whom he had been associated at various times in the course of his life. His observations on the peculiar methods of the different artists whom he had seen at work are very interesting. How characteristic are the pictures which we find in one of these letters of the manner in which Turner, Wilkie, and Haydon, went to work, each bringing out in some manner peculiar to himself his wonderful effects!

LETTERS TO W. DAVISON, ESQ., HARTLEPOOL.

Haughton Cottage, near Darlington,
Nov. 23rd, 1845.

MY DEAR DAVISON,—It is quite delightful to hear from you again. Mrs. Bewick and myself are much concerned for Mrs. Davison, that she still continues to be a sufferer; certainly the air of the sea-coast must be too strong for her. I am quite sure that it is so for me, or we should have been down to the sea-side not unfrequently this summer, for the benefit of a change; but my health, although at present pretty good, is so precarious and delicate that a *dry* and sheltered situation seems necessary, and the place where we are now is extremely so. Indeed, this place has been called by physicians 'the Montpelier of the North.' We live upon sand and gravel, and the moisture is absorbed rapidly. Collins, the landscape-painter, was the same, and he was ordered to remove to Hampstead to a dry sub-soil, and I believe he is living there still. The air here is mild, and the situation so sheltered that vegetables are ready in the season three weeks or a month earlier even than in Darlington, which is only a mile distant.

Miss Ada, I have no doubt, will be a 'sonsie' lassie. Let her draw *everything* except French specimens of chalk drawing, as they are very 'mannered.' He who would be a draughtsman must draw from the round, beginning with hands and feet and heads, or parts of these; but it requires great application. I drew for half a year, every day labouring and sighing to produce what I saw before me. But it is very different with a young lady who wishes only for an accomplishment. I should recommend her to draw trees, ships, rocks, clouds, waters, plants, or railing, as well as parts of the figure. I mean drawing from nature out-of-doors, for her health as well as practice, exercising the hand and eye. *Application*—application—application, is the thing, Miss Ada Davison; and therefore I would have it partly out-of-doors.

In this place I have not a single plaster cast, but probably at Newcastle some hands or feet or heads may be had. Mr. Quelch has everything of this kind at his house; he brought them from London; and I have no doubt but that he would willingly lend anything to you. A hand, and foot, and head, would be quite enough for some time, and they ought to be drawn in chalk the full size, in every possible view. I began to draw upon common cartridge paper, with black and white chalk, and had some difficulty in getting the outline and proportions. A few outlines merely will be very good to begin with — the full size; and never mind how rude, say some encouraging words to induce more trials. When I began I had never seen a port-crayon, and often had not the means to buy bread to rub out with; but nothing deterred me. Neither hunger nor declining health prevented me from beginning at five o'clock in the morning, and working till twelve o'clock at night, until I had mastered the difficulties; and this application told so much upon me, that my legs were swollen, and I had to keep them upon a chair while I worked, until I was told that confinement was killing me. But I had mastered the beginning, and looked onward, little dreaming of that future of which Hazlitt spoke to the boy at Dulwich College.

I am glad you keep painting, and, with all due deference to Miss Ada, I must say that your department—landscape—is the most pleasurable. I should like to see some of your recent works. Wilkie's 'Village Festival' must have been a very laborious undertaking, but I have no doubt that you have made a beautiful copy, although I confess to you this is not a picture that I like so well as many of his other works. The figures always strike me as being small for the size of the picture, and so not sufficiently prominent, and leaving a good deal of space to be filled by other material. It may be considered something between a landscape and a figure picture, and is neither the one nor the other, although the subject is one in which the figures ought to be the all-important part. The copy you made from would be Burlison's, no doubt; and a very good copy it seemed to me, and one that I should like

BEWICK'S RESIDENCE. 143

to possess. You were lucky to get hold of the sketch of Constable's, and in a frame it will be delightful.

I have not been from home for a length of time. I am obliged to keep as quiet as possible, and I assure you to live here is to be as quiet and retired as any tired person need wish to be. The house I live in was built by myself for the purpose of letting, but I came here because my health required retirement. We have not got all complete in the inside, as my painting affairs throw certain parts into confusion. I make the best room into a studio (not a very good one), and the room adjoining contains paints, canvas, and a heterogeneous mass of pictures and frames, &c. &c. Our living room is to your taste, I dare say; the whole of the walls are covered with old pictures on a crimson paper; the furniture is of carved oak. My Vandyck is over the fireplace, in a beautiful light. I paint an occasional portrait or fancy head. I was employed lately to paint a portrait of one of the Carmelite nuns, with a very picturesque and interesting costume—that, literally, of the ancient Spanish peasant, which they wear to this day without the slightest modification. It is the portrait of a lady who paints and draws. She has travelled often in Italy, and all over the world, and, although now a nun, is an extremely interesting person. Mrs. Davison may imagine me—the palette on my thumb, in the nursery, surrounded by nuns, veiled, with musical voices, and some young, interesting, and beautiful, with this picturesque costume, and sandalled feet. Mrs. Bewick desires her kindest regards to Mrs. and Miss Davison and yourself, in which I beg to join, and am, my dear Davison,

Yours truly,
W. BEWICK.

Haughton Cottage, Jan. 15th, 1850.

MY DEAR DAVISON,—With all due decorum I begin my long-delayed note to you by wishing a happy new year to you, not forgetting Miss Ada; who I hope, and do not doubt, will add to every other cause of happiness in store for you both, and all three.

My friend Miss Quelch has told Mrs. Bewick that you intended to write to me, so I take the will for the deed, and have no doubt that you are prevented by the usual causes, procrastination, or too much 'of that same' writing in the ledger, daily accounts, &c. To me, I confess, in my younger days, this was 'the hatred of my soul,' and, indeed, now, after all the romance of life is over, and I am settled down in a staid country retirement, with nothing to do, I still make a stumblingblock of this 'keeping accounts,' and do it as little as possible. I regard this as a weakness, and always think it a defect in my organisation, or lack of the faculty of calculation. I am glad to let my wife be the money-keeper, the payer of bills, and the buyer of everything, except bricks and wood. No doubt, then, you will wonder how I get through my time. I do as well as I can; and tell Mrs. Davison I endeavour to laugh as much, and as often, as I can get an opportunity for exhibiting the risible expression of my now old-looking visage,—old with so many years of dire experience and buffeting with difficulties (in art), and the seriousness, if not the peevishness, of mankind. I amuse myself by looking out into the little world around me, and diving into character, real or pretended, and finding out innumerable little curiosities, all highly edifying in their way; and these I sometimes put on paper.

'Well,' you will say, 'this is about anything rather than art.' Really, Sir, I never talk about the arts at all, simply because here there is no one to talk to on that particular subject. It comes upon me as quite a new thing, a novelty, and I can hardly get hold of the usual terms and expressions belonging to the mystery, —such as, the 'subtleties,' 'manipulations,' and other German novelties in the code of art-language. I am quite at a loss how to commence with you on this our old score. I hear you constantly paint and draw; and I want to know if you still have the enjoyment of pleasing yourself with your greys, and browns, and half-tints?—your 'bit' of positive in a sea of 'breadth?' I see you, on a certain day, very busy; with Mrs. Davison full of admiration at everything you do, which is the delight of life! We shall be together again some of these days, I hope (I mean you and I, and our two wives).

Mrs. Bewick joins me in earnest regards to

both of you, and to Miss Ada; and in the hope of having good news from you,

I am, my dear Davison, yours very truly,

WILLIAM BEWICK.

P.S.—I inclose you a very beautiful prospectus of a work proposed to be published by that very ingenious and extremely clever artist and friend of mine (perhaps of yours also), Mr. Archer; the intimate friend of Balmer, and the author of the short memoir of him in the *Art-Union,* at the time of his death. Mr. Archer and Mr. Lance married sisters. The author of the work on London is an extremely clever draughtsman and engraver, and writes in a very nice, understandable style. He is member of and lecturer at the Archæological Societies, and therefore well educated and fit to carry out the beautiful work he is now about. He has Prince Albert, and a host of noblemen and *dilettanti* subscribers.

CHAPTER VI.

CONTINUATION OF CORRESPONDENCE WITH MR. DAVISON — A FRIEND OF KEATS THE POET — ADVICE TO HIS FRIEND — MR. SEVERN — PYNE THE ARTIST — PORTRAIT OF MARY BENTON — EXHIBITION OF HIS CARTOONS DESIRED AT NEW YORK — TURNER — REMINISCENCES OF GREAT ARTISTS — LETTERS TO MRS. DAVISON.

Haughton-le-Skerne, near Darlington,
Nov. 17th, 1850.

MY DEAR DAVISON,—I have your two nice and chatty letters. The first came when I was from home, painting an extraordinarily aged person. What do you think of one hundred and nineteen years?—a face all wrinkles and puckers! I painted two pictures from this person; one is a front face, and the other a profile.

I am now building a house in which I shall have a good gallery for my cartoons from Michael Angelo, that are at present rolled up, and have not seen the light for ten years.

Your imaginary bliss as a picture-dealer I can well understand, and fancy you scrubbing and rubbing up some antique Van Spruggen or Signor Linkermfeedle, and after you have taken away with 'essence of salt,' or 'spike lavender,' whatever there might have been of good on the canvas, delighted to see how 'fresh' it is, how new-looking and clear of dirt, as they say, and that you had indeed got to its original state, 'pure as it was when just painted!' and so forth. You then spend days filling up cracks and holes, matching the colour and varnishing, and crown the accumulated sin by blandly asserting the name of the original artist, say Claude, or Waterloo, or, perhaps, Vandeveldt: is this endurable? Oh! I have seen these dealers spoiling, scrubbing, smoking, and swaggering, spending perhaps five or six days in skinning a picture, and most valuable and national works spoiled by these pretenders. All artists have a just horror for these chapmen; they certainly do come in contact with gentlemen connoisseurs, and often rule them; but their pleasure in art is only in proportion to the gain they make by it, and it is astonishing what influence some of these fellows have over gentlemen of real feeling for art merely by their swagger and appearance.

But, to turn to something else, I am truly glad to learn that you are determined to spare nothing in the perfecting of Miss Davison's education. Speaking of education puts me in mind of an old friend who married, and is come into the possession of a large family, and who has written to me describing his children, and how they are advancing themselves. He is a poor artist, but rich in affection and talents, industrious, and a gentleman. I only need say that Mr. Severn was the friend of Keats the poet, and tended him until his death at Rome. His tenderness and affection for the poet was as strong as the love of woman; and as I knew Keats, poor fellow, I now love my friend Severn, and rejoice to see how he has pushed his family forward with nothing but his pencil to help him. He is as honourable and dear a fellow as ever breathed, with a noble and generous spirit, and the feeling of a true gentleman.

My gallery for the cartoons will be 30 feet long by 18 feet wide, and 15 or 16 feet high;

and my painting-room 20 feet by 15 feet. All to be ready to move into it by May-day next, as I have let my present abode from that time. Mrs. Bewick desires me to convey through you her kind regards to Mrs. and Miss Davison, in which I beg to join heart and hand, and am, my dear Davison,

Yours very truly,
W. BEWICK.

Haughton-le-Skerne, Dec. 7th, 1850.

MY DEAR DAVISON,—I should like to see your Rembrandts very much, but had rather they were original things. I cannot but long that you should be doing, what in your own peculiar line you do so well, those delightful bits of sea-side scenes. Why not combine some extraordinary effects in nature, of colour, or light and shadow, taking for your material the objects and forms you know so well, and can draw with such correctness and propriety? You would certainly do something fine in this way, some effects of sky, broad and true to nature. Cattermole did some fine things with Rembrandtist effects and colour; but then he does not paint in oil, and his things are in water-colour, a material not quite so manageable as oil. Now, Turner's are extraordinary works, but then the effects are imaginary, and one cannot reconcile them in any way to our ideas of truth and nature; and hence the difficulty, or rather the impossibility, of this being satisfactory, or truly pleasurable, to the eye, or even to the fancy. I speak only to Turner's latter works, for his early productions are very superior in all the requisites of pictorial harmony, truth, and execution.

My dear *Willie!* (as Mrs. Davison says) do be constant (don't be ashamed at the word) to your *sea*-scapes. Give us every pictorial variety your imagination is capable of. Be most extraordinary, most eccentric, in your productions; but then *do*—do!—what you *can* so easily, and harmonise it to nature, or the appearance or possibility of nature; do this with constancy, and I will warrant you will surprise and delight everybody you care about pleasing.

You ask me about Severn. Mr. Severn is well known in the arts; he was resident in Rome when I was. He paints pictures historical and poetical, and has a fine imaginative fancy, and does some things charmingly. He has been greatly patronised in high quarters. He painted such subjects as 'The Vintage' to admiration, and the King of the Belgians bought one of these admirable works at a great price. He is also a poet and musician, composing and playing on the piano, his own music. Dear, dear Davison! here I am; can do nothing, as Hazlitt used to say of himself—'Damn it, nothing, Sir;' and when he missed a ball at rackets, he shouted in despair, 'Sheer incapacity, by G—.'

Ever yours most truly,
W. Bewick.

Michael Angelo Gallery!!!
Haughton-le-Skerne, near Darlington,
June, 1851.

My dear Davison,—Happiest of mortals, you have seen everything the metropolis of the world contains in 1851! And now for once I do envy you. I do covet your opportunity, your leisure, and your discriminating selection of all the choicest products of nature or art, and at every symposium at which you feasted.

I cannot follow you in your remarks on the works of artists. You speak highly of Pyne. He is a very superior artist, and, at the same time, a remarkably clever man, and as to theory, will outrun you (theorist out-and-out) in nostrums, and propositions, and experiments, and ifs, and buts, and whys, and wherefores, and all the jingle of right angle, triangle, A B C, &c. &c. It appears that you were at Sunderland just a day too soon, for the day after the Doctor received the profile portrait of Mary Benton, the old woman of whom I spoke in a former letter. The other picture which I painted of this fine old lady has been engraved in the *Illustrated London News*, and there is an account of her obtained from the gentleman who purchased the portrait. I will send you (for lack of news) a note from the proprietor of the picture—Mr. Fox, of Westbourne Terrace, Hyde Park—into whose collection it has found its way. Indeed, he wrote to me to inquire if I would part with the picture. I named my London price for it, and when he received it he was good enough to send me a cheque upon Coutts for double the amount. Several artists have written to congratulate me upon this successful production, particularly the hands, expression, &c. You will be good enough to return the notes to me, and of course you must consider them confidential. My gallery progresses, and is nearly finished. If it were dry enough, my cartoons would be up in a twinkling, and then, 'my dear fellow!' you will be no longer excused. I have some good rooms in my new house, although they are all wet, except a little breakfast-room and bed-room, which are dry, and in which we keep rattling fires every day, so making an increase in the coal-trade.

Mrs. Bewick desires me to convey to Mrs. and Miss Davison her kindest regards, as well as to yourself, in which I beg to join, and am, my dear Davison,

Yours very truly,
W. Bewick.

Haughton-le-Skerne, near Darlington,
Jan. 2nd, 1852.

My dear Davison,—Here is 1852. What do we promise ourselves in the shape of work? Are you looking forward to exercising your brush at all? I am in great anxiety about my cartoons, as they are beginning to mildew from the damp, although I have a large fire in the flue night and day. I fear they will have to be taken down, and from the straining frames. How grand they look! I have ten stretched, and five in frames. The Americans want to have them in their forthcoming Exhibition at New York, but the guarantee is not sufficient for me; and, besides, I would like it better that they remained in this country somewhere secured, as most probably no other copies will ever be made, by reason of the great expense and difficulty, and I am told the frescoes are much decayed since mine were done. Now, Sir Davison! be in good humour with me, make my genteelest bow to the ladies, and do tell me how Mrs. Davison is, as Mrs. Bewick will be anxious to know; and I send this off by the post, in the hope that it will reach you before all the merry-making and Christmas cheer are ended.

Yours, very truly,
My dear Davison,
W. BEWICK.

Haughton House, near Darlington,
Feb. 3rd, 1853.

MY DEAR DAVISON,—Having written a few days ago to Mrs. Davison when in a very sullen and moody humour, and feeling myself rather lively and spirited to-day, I take it into my head to talk to you in the serious and prosaic way most suitable to our usual subject, the Arts. I am sprightly because I am just left alone, after being cheered up by two bright ladies shining in their satins — Quakeresses, with as fine bred horses and trappings to their carriage as any nobleman in this fair England. The coachman has a modest living. How these fair Quakeresses have laughed! What happy faces, beaming with goodness, telling of good cheer and happy homes! My wife is gone out, albeit it snows, and I am free for a gossip with you.

Your two last notes lie before me. I should like, indeed, to see your experiments *à la Turner*. I must beg to inform you that I have myself seen my friend Turner paint, and and that too upon some of his finest works. You say no one was ever let into his secret by seeing him paint, but seeing him paint would not let you or me into his secret. Indeed, he did not know that he had a secret. To know how he painted when he was thirty or forty would be the desideratum of those who play follow-my-leader. Although so very close in money affairs, he was a cordial old chap. I was never introduced to him, but he came boldly up to me and held out his (extraordinary) hand, and being, as I am, a judge of shakes, his shake told me his character, and we thereupon gave a double shake. He was very pleasant, and you would have been mighty fond of him, but you could have seen no rainbow or prismatic colours in him or in his costume. His complexion was of a very healthy hue, as if mellowed by the sun and fine weather, like ripe corn. Indeed, there is a friend of mine at Sunderland, the very man, in figure, face, and complexion, and about the age; so that, if ever you want to see how Turner looked, our Doctor can contrive you a meeting, and he is just as likely to surprise and astonish you with his extraordinary effects in his way as the real Turner. Indeed, the painter was as natural and simple as any real landscape, and did not look as if he represented 200,000*l*.

But, seriously, I have seen Turner paint, Wilkie paint, and of course Haydon (although I was the only painter, or pupil, or student allowed to be present while he was at work), and Landseer, with some others of not equal eminence in the executive or effective departments of the art; and I cannot say that any *scumbled* at the rate you speak of, although Turner had a very curious and almost unaccountable process of bringing up the ultimate perfection of his tones and effects. I suppose you would like vastly to hear me describe their methods—secrets if you will—but, my dear Sir, what an inquiry it would be — to what fearful discussion would it lead — the analysing the palettes of each of these eminent painters, after they have been painting a few hours. Nobody could suppose that Wilkie could produce execution so near perfection from such a furbished up palette, the scrapings, the savings, and the skin, with just a bit of the surface rubbed clean to wet his pencil on and mix his tints. His palette was a save-all, with bits of tints of colour remaining for days and weeks.

Then, as to Haydon, his palette — but why bother you in this way, who enjoy the imagination, the unreal, the mystery of men's ways in their studio? If you knew exactly how, why, and wherefore, it would prevent the exercising your invention and imaginative faculties, stop the experiments that you so delight in, and delight everybody else with. I say again I should like very much to see some of those Turners of yours, either the Italian ones or that 'sea-storm' that is now left in your head, and was so sublimely exhibited before your eyes a few days ago in fearful reality. I have never seen Burnett's work; but Turner's early works are upon a different principle to his last. Which do you like best? We wish we were nearer you, by 'earthquakes' or any other process. Mrs. Be-

wick joins me in kind regards to Mrs., Miss,
Davison, and yourself, and

  I am, my dear Davison,
    Yours very sincerely,
      W. BEWICK.

Not the least pleasing peculiarity in the correspondence of Bewick is its variety, passing with perfect ease from grave to gay, from discussions on art to the ordinary details of domestic life. After the more serious letters which he had written to Mr. Davison, the following letters to that gentleman's wife afford us delightful specimens of his lighter and more sportive mood :—

    Haughton House, near Darlington,
      July 21st, 1853.

MY DEAR MRS. DAVISON,—I do bless that blarney-stone with all my heart, no matter by what name it goes. I had it very racy and sweet when I was in old Ireland in my youth, in the mild South, where the hot sun melts the icy hearts of both men and women. In the north I own to its rarity. I am chilled by the rigidity and the sternness of so cold a phlegm as reigns in these Northern regions; and when something that smacks of heart-warmth comes to our deadened finger-ends, there is a tingle all over one's nervous sensibility, quite unusual, and one cannot help asking what it means,—how?—where are we?—is it real?—does it come from a southern or northern latitude; and we remain in a maze of pleasant sensations; and I for one do not care a straw, why, or whence, or how you call it, civility, amenity, or other fine names in the catalogue,—no, I meant to say category of pleasurable sensations.

But mine, Mrs. Davison, is a curious fatality. I love the South, the Southern people, the refinements of a Southern hemisphere, arts, literature, science, the natural frankness and generosity accompanying high attainments and the possession of great genius bestowed upon the few. And look at me! I am thrown into a place here where, literally speaking, there is not one individual being that possesses the slightest inclination or taste for any of the humanising accomplishments. Here is a cold humid atmosphere—cold people, who take a poet for an exciseman, a painter for a fellow not to be trusted further than ready money will take him, and who, astonished to find that an author who has amused them at a feast is only an author, exclaim, 'We thought he had been a gentleman!' And a gentleman he was, ma'am, as well bred as any of them, though he had stooped to literature, and now enjoys a world-wide fame, known to these Northern folk by his exuberant wit and original genius; and we boast of him as the author of *Vanity Fair*, the Thackeray, and my friend. Mrs. Bewick desires her love to you all, and so does, my dear Mrs. Davison,

Yours truly,
W. BEWICK.

Haughton House, near Darlington,
August 24th, 1853.

MY DEAR MRS. DAVISON,—We have, it seems, reciprocated thoughts, for Mrs. Bewick and myself have often wondered how Mr. Davison was going on, and I have procrastinated, ma'am, from day to day, hugging the delightful satisfaction of having shirked a duty, avoided a pleasure, until your note this morning 'brings me up to the scratch;'—scratchy enough my hand is, for I never could write an 'office' hand, although I have whilom tried. Hazlitt used to say, 'He liked to see how painters formed their tottering letters,' and I have heard a fine landscape-painter swear a tremendous oath at these words, and offer to write with any man living for one hundred pounds; and he showed me his handwriting, which was certainly beautiful. Alas! both these great spirits are in the dust. Is my dear William mad,—to walk seven miles, and remain in bed next day? Is it possible that an old business-man like my friend William should do such a mad freak? Had I done it, it would have been nothing to surprise anybody, a harum-scarum fellow like me, that gets on to the moon and off again, rides on the thistle-down, blowing bubbles to the winds of heaven, and nobody thinks it strange; they only wink, and point, and say, 'Ah! he—he's west-north-west,' and leave me to my dreams and vagaries.

Well, Mrs. D., have you read that extraordinary book by Mrs. Crow, *The Night Side of Nature?* If you have not, get it; it is quite in your way; it will take you to the seventh heaven, and more. I am at present going through it. I have not taken any of the cherry-bark, because I have none; but I have been going on pretty well without any drugs whatever; and now it is fine weather, I get out as much as my frame will bear, and go to bed after dinner, which refreshes me. I avoid all invitations out, and deny myself the pleasure of fine dinners and pleasant company, even in this village. Though a lady desired to drive me in her carriage three miles off to a delightful dinner, I had the heart to refuse the risk. What does my friend William say to this self-denial?—*he* could not do it. Everybody wants to drive me off to try change of air, but I think of the comforts of home, and cannot, as yet, make up my mind.

I must tell you of the arrival of a marble bust of me from Rome. It came last week, and was found dropped outside my gate early one morning by the servant. The woman tried to carry me, but could not. You may rely upon it, I was in a flurry when told in bed where my other head was lying, being sure the nose would be broken off, or that some mutilation would disfigure it; and when it was brought into the house, I heard,—nay, I felt that something or other was knocking about in the inside of the case. I exclaimed 'It is the nose! depend upon it;' and we were all impatient to open it and see. It was delightful to see how it was packed, so secure and safe; and when it was at last got fairly out, Mrs. Bewick exclaimed, 'How beautiful!' and kissed its cold lips. The bust is by the great sculptor Gibson, my friend. It was modelled twenty-five years ago, and cut in marble in 1853—mind, not at all by my desire. Gibson, in the first place, asked me to sit to him. The model was seen in Rome by some friends, and a drawing of it brought over for Mrs. Bewick by a lady, and they have persuaded her to get it done in marble. Everybody exclaims, How beautiful it is! I must say as a work of art it is quite equal to the antique. It is lifesize. Our kind regards to William and Ada, and I am,

My dear Mrs. Davison,

Yours truly,

W. BEWICK.

Haughton, near Darlington,
Sept. 9th, 1853.

DEAR MRS. DAVISON,—As I am desirous not to lose Gibson's note, I write for fear that you should have forgotten that it was my wish that it should be returned. Indeed, my having occasion to show it to a friend of Gibson's who paid me a visit yesterday, put me in mind that it was at Hartlepool, and I thought it better to write to you in case it had escaped your memory.

There is a strange and unexpected revelation quoted from Tom Taylor's Autobiography of Haydon inserted in the *Durham Advertiser* of this day. When I read the quotation, it brought back the dim remembrance of those early days. Of course, I got through it with palpitating heart, for I had great difficulty to manage my feelings. Little did I think it would ever be recorded in the language of the moment. When we consider the extraordinary circumstances under which Haydon painted the figure of Lazarus, it often occurs to me what wonderful powers of mind were possessed by this man; for be it known to you that he has recorded his being arrested at that time ; and in the middle of his work, he was again arrested two separate times. I was mounted upon a box, upon a chair, upon a table ; and when he came back a third time and mounted the steps, he said to me in accents not to be forgotten, 'Bewick, if I am called out again, it will be impossible for me to go on; that is the third time this morning that I have been arrested.' He painted the head, hands, and drapery all in that day! and it has never been touched since. Sir Walter Scott told me, whilst looking at the picture, that it was a perfect realisation of what he himself imagined when reading the account in the Bible. I hope Mr. Davison continues to improve and to be prudent. I am going on pretty well at present. Mrs. Bewick joins with me in our kind regards to Ada, William, and yourself, and

I am, my dear Mrs. Davison,
Yours very truly,
W. BEWICK.

CHAPTER VII.

CORRESPONDENCE WITH MR. DAVISON CONTINUED—LEIGH HUNT, KEATS, AND HAYDON—'GROUNDS' OF THE OLD PAINTERS—HAYDON'S AUTOBIOGRAPHY—HIS ABSURD THEORIES—GREEK AND GOTHIC ARCHITECTURE—THE CARTOONS BY NIGHT-LIGHT—EXHIBITION OF ART-TREASURES AT MANCHESTER—EXHIBITION OF FRENCH PICTURES AT NEWCASTLE—LANDSCAPE-PAINTING—A FAVOURITE GREEN—REMINISCENCE OF FLORENCE—THE TURNER GALLERY—MEETING WITH AN OLD FRIEND—RABY CASTLE.

Haughton-le-Skerne, near Darlington,
Oct. 12th, 1853.

MY DEAR DAVISON,—I am very much obliged to you for sending me the nice, freely written letter from the Lakes. I remember the time when I was at Sir John Leicester's gallery to view the fine collection of modern works. It is, indeed, a long, long time ago, and I remember I was there in company with Mr. Leigh Hunt, Keats and Haydon, the Landseers, and others.

Mr. Haydon had asked permission to take this party; and Sir John gave orders that when he and his party came he should be informed. He and Lady Leicester and their friends came in to see those remarkable men, and we all were introduced (a very unusual thing on such occasions). Lady Leicester was beautiful, and there was a full-length portrait of her by Sir Thomas Lawrence, equally beautiful. Looking at me she asked Mr. Haydon if all his pupils had black hair (the Landseers have all flaxen polls); and when I read Mr. F.'s remark about my 'black hair,' it brought the circumstance to my mind. Leigh Hunt had a profusion of black hair at that time, and he was pale, and altogether a remarkable-looking man, with a searching, dark, and beaming eye, and everybody seemed struck with his uncommon and intellectual appearance. Keats and Haydon were not so tall, but both remarkable in their appearance. With our united love to you, William, and Ada,

I am, dear Davison,

Yours very truly,

W. BEWICK.

Haughton-le-Skerne,
Oct. 21st, 1853.

My dear Davison,—Your note written on the 18th duly came to me this morning. This brings me to the 'chromatic scale' again, and I wish very much you would fulfil your promise of supplying me with your recently discovered improvements, together with a plan of them. That the grounds of the old painters are known as to colour is pretty correct; but what 'grounds' have you for supposing that they laid those grounds on a principle of contrast? It seems very like saying, I shall prove my argument by the power of contradiction. The Dutch masters had a white ground. Then, supposing that Rembrandt painted in a head or other subject *at once*, or Rubens—both of whom, it is known, often did so—how could they have a chromatic or 'accidental' ground for such pictures, painting in red under blue, purple under yellow, and so on? The fact that the Venetians painted upon a brilliant system of glazing cannot be a part of this chromatic principle, although I have seen Titian copied by laying in the *whole* in grey; but there was a very different reason for this, seeing that the under-colour in the original was *cooler* than the upper transparent glazing.

Here is the first volume of Haydon's Autobiography brought in to me, so I shall have a feast, I guess. Only fancy twenty-seven folio volumes for his journal! His correspondence, it appears, is not published in the life, but very probably will come afterwards. Of all lives, 'autobiography' is the most interesting. Benvenuto Cellini's is a romance that no fancy or imagination could have invented. It is interesting, because he writes of his feelings, his peculiarities, and his habits. He takes you to the time in which he lived — to the home, the place, his acquaintances, enemies and friends, his occupations, his successes, his difficulties, anxieties, sufferings, pleasures, loves, and disappointments. And although this may be egotism, when years are past and another generation has come, it has grown into the interest of history, and is a valuable illustration of the state of society at that particular period.

And now, my dear Davison, I have had my chat with you, and will turn to my old master and see him again as he lived. Mrs. Bewick unites with me in kind regards to you and all that to you do belong.

And I am, my dear William,

Yours very truly,

W. BEWICK.

The following letter is of great interest, as containing Bewick's judgment on the master who had been so friendly to him in the early part of his career. These remarks were occasioned by the appearance of Haydon's Autobiography:—

Haughton-le-Skerne, near Darlington,
Nov. 20th, 1853.

MY DEAR MRS. DAVISON,—I suppose you will have read Haydon's memoir by this time. Everybody is reading it, and everybody is reviewing it. I have just finished the third volume, and I suppose the second edition is required, which will be corrected and improved; so if you have not yet read it, wait for the second edition. The third volume gives me some acid falsities which I think I ought to correct, either in the papers or some other way. I should not like to reflect upon the memory of one who seems to have had everybody upon him, who, like most other men, was not quite perfection, but had many fine qualities, and very great genius and intellectual power. If these had only been kept quite devoted to the great task for which he was fitted, his noble efforts might have astonished the world and honoured his country. We may indulge in the speculation that the painter of the finest work of high art in this country, 'The Judgment of Solomon,' must, under favourable circumstances, have achieved things which would have done honour to the country and to our School of Art. But after the painting of 'Lazarus,' when a terrible pecuniary embarrassment beset him, and his canvas could only obtain divided attentions, while his mind was 'ill at ease,' and anxieties frittered away noble genius, what wonder though life became a burden intolerable? As it was, under all the unfavourable circumstances, he earned, by his industry and talent, at the rate of 500*l.* per annum, or more; yet he could not keep the bailiffs out of the house! Some years he cleared from a thousand to two thousand. Mrs. Bewick and myself hope you are all well, and we unite in our loves to you, and I am,

My dear Mrs. Davison,
Yours truly,
W. BEWICK.

Haughton, Dec. 6th, 1853.

MY DEAR DAVISON,—I shall set you down as 'the silent man,' or 'the narrow-necked bottle' of Shakespeare. You go to Paris, and I hear nothing of it from you until the pith and marrow of your impression is retailed in gossip to the nobodies of every day, and utterly frittered away. You pass up to London, and not a word you have to tell me of anything that either pleases or displeases you. It appears you rave about the Turners; you have gloated upon them; and you have set up poor old ruddy-faced Turner as 'the god of your idolatry.' Of course I want to know all about your impressions before they evaporate, and leave only perhaps faint the steam of your effervescence anent this old conundrum; and as a contribution to the hodge-podge you keep boiling and bubbling in the cook-shop of your brain-pan. I send you a curious revelation about pictures in Queen Anne Street. If you have not seen it before, it will interest you as to the materials Turner put into some of the examples of his genius, and his grudging parsimony with regard to finery in his mansion. In an appendix to Haydon's Life, vol. iii., there is a copy of Sir Joshua's memorandum of his colours and pigments; the wax and balsams he brushed on his canvases, with Beechey's and Haydon's notes upon the same. To you, who are scientifically and chemically hodge-podgy, and up to the gamut of chromatic tinctures, the airy evanescences of light, or the Rembrandtish darkness of scene, of the colours that stand, and those that *turn* to airy nothing, of all the vehicles that are good, who know all about table-turning, this knowledge of Turner's use of materials will be marvellously interesting.

My life has been a life of frankness, but I sometimes like to be as dry and mysterious as any clockmaker or barber-politician. I try to mystify and wrap up simples in a labyrinth, or to tie them in a true-lover's knot, that can only be cut by the short 'twig' of a woman's eye. I had a bold tenant once, a hero who told some one that he did not like a smiling landlord (meaning me). Ever since that I have tried to look serious, grave, or sour, as business men seem to do, even if they are only selling a ha'porth of needles or a twopenny doll, a child's cradle or little Tommy's rattle.

But to return to Sir Joshua. What a melancholy thing it is to think that he should have pestered his mind with such abominable theories and humbugs of practice as are recorded in his memoranda! And what a fickleness he exhibits in so many times changing and experimenting, and at every change he writes down that he is 'stabilito in muno,' &c. This repeatedly occurs, and is as often changed again by new and unheard-of experiments.

My wife desires her kind regards to you, Mrs. Davison, and all, in which I beg most cordially to join, and I am,

My dear Mrs. Davison,
Yours sincerely,
W. BEWICK.

Haughton, Dec. 17th, 1853.

My dear Davison,—I have, then, done what I wished,—made you speak out in four sheets of note-paper. Anything is better than bottling all your blue ink in self-possession and passive silence. I am equally an admirer of Greek architecture, Turner, and Sir Joshua, and cannot turn over to Mr. Ruskin all at once. The critics say that Haydon was insane (never was there a greater mistake), and now they say Ruskin is over the moon. I have not read his *Stones of Venice*, nor his remarks about Turner, except by snatches and odd bits. Setting aside fine writing, I do not see why one may not admire Greek architecture and Gothic at the same time, without running to the extremes of determined hatred and rapturous attachment. Each possesses its peculiar merits, fitness, and beauty; comparison and preference of one or other serves no object. They will still exist to the admiration of all posterity. It is something like the dispute about the superiority of Shakespeare and Milton, Michael Angelo and Raphael. I warrant you there is something superlatively good in all. Wherefore should we not feel the beautiful harmony and purity, the just proportions and classic taste of Greek architecture? Are we to be tied down to accept impressions of one man's mind, when taste is the guiding influence? Surely I may be impressed with the solemnity — sublimity, if you will — of a venerable Gothic structure, without being thereby disqualified from perceiving the beauty of another equally harmonious, but of a distinct character of architecture? And, without pretending to any knowledge of the character of Mr. Ruskin's mind, there does surely seem something very peculiar in that he sees nothing good in architecture but in Gothic structures, nothing so perfect in art or so wonderful as Turner's pictures! Surely, Mr. Davison, there are certain qualities of colour surpassing every other painter in the landscapes of Titian, in those of Giorgioni rich and deep harmony, and in those of Salvator Rosa a power of handling, a vigour and truth, and, what is more, a distinctive character in his forms, in his touches, and in his foliage, that Turner, with all his excellencies, never attempted.

I doubt that I am becoming serious, and that will not do. So now you see me smile, and I am reflective, as one is when treading on delicate and tender ground. Mrs. Bewick desires to unite with me in kind regards to Mrs. Davison and yourself; and I am, dear Davison,

Yours, very sincerely,
W. BEWICK.

Haughton-le-Skerne, near Darlington,
July 16th, 1854.

MY DEAR DAVISON,—I am, and so are all our folks, sorry that you could not get up the steam sufficiently to be here at our party, particularly as my cartoons looked better than ever I saw them before. Night-light is the thing for them; it throws a glow and tone over them that an eye accustomed to the richness of oil-painting feels wanting in fresco. There is all the force and power peculiar to fresco, and the tone of an artificial light that enriches its dryness. I could have wished to give you longer notice of my intention of lighting them up, but I only thought of it the day before, and the chandeliers only arrived just in time from Darlington. It was quite an experiment. It was pretty nearly a rout; and when the folks paired off into the gallery, surprise and wonder seemed to be the effect of the extraordinary beings that started from the walls as if into life,—a gigantic race, with extraordinary expressions and grand solemnity, that seemed, indeed, to awe the spectators. Imagine the contrast: coming out of the drawing-room costumed in modern elegance, with social smiles, and stepping at once among the Prophets and Sibyls of patriarchal times, the embodiments of supernatural intelligence!

Everybody I meet now asks to see these wonderful things. Their effect is magical, it appears, for I have never shown them here in their present completeness before.

Fortunately for myself and for my visitors, I keep up pretty well, but cannot go very far from home; for if I step over the mark of a mile or so, I am obliged to go to bed on my return; and I cannot go out to parties of any kind.

With our kind regards to all of you and Miss Quelch, I am, my dear Davison,

    Yours, very truly,
      W. Bewick.

    Haughton House, near Darlington,
      Jan. 1st, 1857.

My dear Davison,—I write to wish you and yours a happy new year, and many returns of the same. I hope you have had a merry Christmas, and that your health, and that of Mrs. Davison, is such as to enable you both to enjoy the good things of this season of the year with all the zest and jollity of your youthful days.

What a fuss there is about our old friend Turner! How he has at last astonished the world of property! What would you not give for a scrap of Turner? Your little finger, I dare say. What would you have given for a shake of that mighty hand? or to have had your eyesight blest with a peep at the giant doing his wondrous work, a sly peep past the curtain to see him handle the brush, to see him poking away at his little shabby palette of dirty colours?

What a wondrous artist Genius is! What a coiner,—what a 'philosopher's stone!' What transmutations it can effect, and how it can make the lieges stare, ope their 'glazed eyes,' and strike their illiterate senses with strange sensations, and pluck admiration from ignorance, envy, or jealousy!

Be good enough to tell Mrs. Davison, with my love to her (if you are not jealous), that I am going on slowly with my recovery, and hope to come round again to something like myself, although lopped of the spring of youth, and my black locks changed to venerable grey. I hope to be well enough to go to Manchester to see 'the Treasures' of Art there. You, of course, will go. Can we hope to meet there? If I can stir up enough of courage to pack up a rubbing in of Turner's, some fine day I will send it to you. It is about two feet long, old and dirty;—a bridge of one arch, high up between two rocks, thrown into shade, with a spurt of water jumping over them. If anything is Turner's, this dash of water is. Mrs. Bewick desires to unite with me in our best regards to

you and to Mrs. and Miss Davison, and I am,
my dear Davison,

Yours truly,

W. Bewick.

Haughton House, near Darlington,
July 11th, 1857.

My dear Davison,—We have just returned from Manchester! I ran all risks, and set off on Monday last, returning last night, so that we had three clear hard-working days. The fatigue has been too much for me, and we returned two days sooner than we intended. My stars! Willie, but if you have not been there yet, what a joy you have to come to! Do not speak of Turner, *there* you have him in all his glory, in oil, in water, in marvellous revelry! Poor, old, farmer-looking fellow—how I love him for his genius!—how I cry 'Bravo' at every wonder of his pencil! Constable is not sufficiently represented. Wilkie's early pictures are capital, his late ones are going to pieces like old ships, cracking so that the cracks cannot be filled up. Here is his 'Hookabiadar,' which cost Mr.

Jacob Bell 150 guineas,—it is quite a marvel how paint could so split up into small square bits, three quarters of an inch square, with wide gaps between. The hand looks as if he had some kind of scale armour on, and people take it for that, or for some peculiarity of the glove. The puff of smoke floating from his mouth, in the background, is quite gone,—it does not exist; and the way it was put in was a fine piece of skill and thought.

Well, sir, there are such Rembrandts, such Vandycks, Titians, Raphaels, in numbers, and in painting quite admirable; and as you gaze upon such marvels, you cry 'Wonderful! wonderful!' as each seems to surpass the other in depth, or breadth, or brilliance, or sleight of hand, or glazing, or power, or transparency, or negative combinations of hues, or vivid and striking identity of character, living, speaking, looking out at you, expecting you to say, 'How do you do?' to them. In these Rembrandt seems glorious. Vandyck, too, is wonderful in flesh, and beauty, and drapery; and so is our Reynolds. Here is his 'Nelly O'Brien,' equal to anybody, beautiful and highly finished, quite an example of lady painting; nothing can be finer, more pure, or powerful, or transparent, or beautiful. What a charm it is! There are some brilliant Titians, and landscape-painters should look at his depth, richness, and brilliance of colour. How he makes the sun shine! Cuyp, and Ruysdael, and Claude are fine. Indeed, this exhibition is a most wonderful one, and the general effect is almost overpowering. Art here is transcendent in every shape ; the paintings are numerous, rich, rare, and of superlative excellence; and though your sense of admiration is roused to the utmost, the study of each picture becomes a laborious task. The noise, the hurry, the bustle, and the crowd, with the music of the organ booming in my ear, afterwards drove away sleep; while the buzz and tumult continued still present to me. On the Thursdays all the fashion of Manchester attend, and everything is genteel and delightfully quiet ; the music is superior, and you have ladies there with costumes costing 150*l*. Now, Davison, you have all the Exhibition, except the English Water Colours; and let me tell you that they surpass the whole world, being wonderfully beautiful, chaste, and elegant. The English school of Art is favourably represented, and stands up well.

Mrs. Bewick's kind regards to Mrs. Davison and Ada, and I am, dear Davison,

Yours truly,

W. BEWICK.

P.S.—There is a donkey painted by me for Haydon—it is the property of Lord de Tabley, and is called Haydon!

Haughton House, near Darlington,
Feb. 21st, 1859.

MY DEAR DAVISON,—We are so glad to see your handwriting again! Have you heard of the exhibition of French pictures at Newcastle? Dr. Burn has sent me a catalogue, but he does not say if they are fine or the contrary. There are many landscapes, and some fine sea-views. One is 'Fishermen hauling a Boat on Shore.' This is a capital subject for you; do try it; you have all the subject with you at Hartlepool, and have not to go to look for it at the 'Dogger Bank' or 'Yarmouth Roads.' I should like very much to see Mr. Burlison's pictures, as I have no doubt they will be full of genius and originality. His *Florence*, is it bright and sunny? I have a delightful memory of Florence and its people, its squares, its statues, its galleries of paintings, and its churches full of interesting art. There seemed nothing there but sun and love! enriched by vineyards and pleasure—with laughter to satiety. I lost myself in Florence, having no map, knowing nothing of the language, and seeking my dinner without knowing the name of the street or of the hotel, or where there was an eating-house, or what to say for 'dinner,' or for the word 'hunger.' Just imagine yourself alone in this predicament, after wandering about in search of churches and pictures all day, not able to find your hotel, nor any friend to speak a word for you, and then, my dear sweet William, you will confess how glorious you are at the town wall, when the nicest of dinners awaits your appetite.

Our love to you all at home, and I am, my dear Davison, yours very truly,

W. BEWICK.

Haughton, Dec. 10th, 1860.

My dear Davison,—I am so glad that you are making yourself happy by pleasing yourself with your work. There is no department of painting so much calculated to give pleasure as landscape (or 'sea-scape') painting. You create your sky,—your effects of light and shadow,—your tone of colour, be it spring, summer, autumn, or winter,—your eye will direct the proper key,—and you work away, lopping or changing, or adding, or bringing out, or hiding in obscurity unfavourable objects; and thus you produce to your educated fancy the breadth and truth of nature. You stand off and view your handiwork with the satisfaction of a superior being,—a creator as far as effects go,—as far as artistic manipulation will carry you; and, as daylight fades, you wish for an hour more of light to complete your work.

Your two pictures mentioned in your last letter will by this time be quite complete, and I shall be glad to learn if you have finished them to your entire satisfaction. Our friend the Doctor mentions your questions about Wilson's beautiful green, whether it has changed to its present purity, or was originally of this particular hue or tint? There can be no doubt that it remains as it was first painted; but if you try to mix any blue and yellow together, you will fail to produce the particular green seen in Wilson's pictures, especially his mid-distance. Now, when I was a young lad at home, and stole to my room by five o'clock on holiday mornings to wrap myself up in seclusion for the day, warm in enthusiasm, and labouring as for some great reward, — with colours, canvasses, and brushes in the most primitive style,—no master,—no adviser,—I was only too glad to seize hold of any little book or pamphlet that might by chance come into my hands; and there did fall into my possession a pamphlet published about the time of Wilson, and mentioning the particular colour to be used for different parts of pictures. I remember very well being delighted with one particular green for different parts of a landscape, which I used, and no mixture that I could invent would produce the delicacy, lightness, and purity of this peculiar green. Many years afterwards I had the opportunity of seeing the landscapes of

Wilson, and then, to be sure, I recognised my old favourite 'green.' You will be surprised to learn that in this early youth I was bold enough to make a large copy of Wilson's 'Niobe' from a print—the colour, of course, all my own. I remember the figures, &c., were highly finished. I took it to London on my first visit, and I had some very great compliments paid to my picture, although it was but a copy. You may imagine my surprise, when I saw the original picture, to find it upon quite a different key to mine, and all the colours of draperies, sky, rocks, and trees quite different. As I studied the peculiarities of colour and breadth of effect from nature, I put in composition my own ideas of colour, and the contrast with the original was very curious indeed.

I have been often told that I ought to have turned my attention to landscape, as that department seemed my peculiar *forte*. However that may be, nothing could give me greater enjoyment than painting a landscape; but my attention and time have been concentrated on work more difficult and more laborious, and, if you like, higher in character. I dare say, what you say of Mr. Burlison's 'Florence' may be correct. I remember Florence, as I saw it and its neighbourhood from a villa a mile distant, built in the midst of vineyards, with a terrace in front looking down upon the city. It was a charming place. On the terrace wall were orange-trees in full bearing, and below nothing but the vine, the olive, the almond, &c., in every direction up to the walls of the city. When I stood upon the terrace for the first time, the city seemed to lie basking in the broad sunlight. It looked as if uninhabited. There was no smoke, nor any of the usual appearances of a town in England, where the canopy of smoke bred by our coal fires keeps us moody and melancholy. The brightness of the town seemed half lost in airy, vapoury heat. All was still, for everybody in it was taking his *siesta*. I felt anxious to make a sketch, but I had been invited to dinner, and to listen to the reading of a manuscript novel that a friend was going to forward to England. So we had much to talk of, and when dinner was over came visitors, two gentlemen and a lady—an English gentleman and his wife, and an Italian Prince. It so happened that the lady was lively and full of enthusiasm. She had sat with her sister very often to Harlow; and, ordering the Prince from the couch, she sat by me to tell me of the extraordinary character of Harlow, whom her father quite idolized. He would come down into the country where they lived and call them all out of bed at two or three o'clock in the morning. Some fine idea had come into his head, and he must have one or both of the sisters up to sit to him. This lady was the most vivacious and quick speaker I ever heard. There was not a moment's pause, and it was delightful to hear her, so sensible were her observations, so well told her anecdotes. This party remained all the evening, so that I spent the night at the villa, sleeping in a grand state-bed, all gold carving and damask. I was enchanted with the view from my window in the morning —the sun dispersing the dew—the city bathed in the most delicate effects of morning colour. As I sauntered through some of the apartments, where there were pictures and statues in abundance, I came to the billiard-room—an extensive hall, with niches all round, filled with marble busts of the Cæsars, &c.; and it seemed to me more like enchantment than reality. I have got a fine, massy new frame for my 'Entombment,' and one for the Velasquez. The effect is mighty fine.

Mrs. Bewick begs to unite with me in our love to Mrs. Davison, Ada, and yourself; and I am, my dear Davison,

Yours truly,
W. BEWICK.

Haughton House, near Darlington,
Jan. 1st, 1861.

MY DEAR DAVISON,—Mrs. Bewick cordially unites with me in wishing you and Mrs. Davison and Ada a happy new year, and many returns of the season. I am glad you know all about the peculiar green that Wilson was in the habit of using, and that is one of the many charms we find in his works.

If you think that I hit off the 'yellow green' in my copy of the print of 'Niobe,' you are quite mistaken. I had at that time never seen a Wilson picture, nor indeed any other picture of any note; I used the green merely because it was a colour I had. I do not think that Wilson got his purity or his aërial effects by their glazing of this colour. As to his greens having changed by using macgilp, if it were so, his blue skies and other pure colours would have changed in like manner. I remember well an exhibition in Bond Street of Glover's own pictures, which were sold by auction, and they were exhibited without frames; alas! I was horrified, they looked so crude, so much green of the gross blue and yellow mixture, and at that time I had a mellowed tone in my eye that ill agreed with Glover's 'painting on the spot.' The wall was full of these gamboge and blue effects; but there were no Wilsons there, as you mention. I am glad you were amused with my account of my visit to the elegant Florentine villa. Mrs. Bewick desires her love to Mrs. Davison; and I am, my dear Davison,

Yours truly,
W. BEWICK.

Haughton House, near Darlington,
Sept. 4th, 1861.

MY DEAR DAVISON,—I write to say that we have arrived all safe, and that I am still alive. We came here on Friday last. As I felt sufficiently recovered from my late severe illness at my brother's at Dagenham, we determined to come home *viâ* London, our object being to see the exhibitions. We were too late for the Royal Academy, and also for Holman Hunt's picture; but we did feast upon the rarities at the National Gallery, the British Institution, and the Kensington Museum. My eye! Davison, but our friend Turner is great at the last place; and, indeed, at the National he compares well. He stands his ground between two of the finest Claudes. Are you not proud that he was an Englishman, and not a Scot or an Irishman? So much noise is made by these latter, that one is glad to find modest merit eclipses all their pretensions, and an Englishman step over their heads by sheer force of genius.

When Turner was painting these glorious works, Sir Walter Scott said to me at Abbotsford, that, 'if we did not mind, the Scotchman would be beating us in the race.' This was in 1824, when Wilkie had painted his best works,—he was at Abbotsford the same time with me. Is it not a triumph to see such wonderful combinations of poetical conception, breadth of treatment, and colour that rivals the brilliancy of the sun? His contrasts also are so masterly and effective. How one revels in the Turner Gallery! what a feast of colour! how the eye is filled with gorgeous effects! what delight he must have felt in pouring out such imaginative creations of his ethereal soul! One is at a loss for language to express one's admiration,—it is so unbounded,—one's feelings, when viewing such exalted and varied emanations of a genius so original and incomparable.

Why, Davison, why don't you go mad when in the Turner Gallery? how do you contain yourself? One should be always alone with Turner, unless one has a companion capable of feeling the magic wonders of his pencil, and thus you can enhance your ecstasy by sympathy in the comprehension of his unrivalled powers. You turn to Landseer, and find wonders of execution, the perfection of manipulation, to which Turner had no pretensions, neither hand nor mind was made for this most beautiful department of the art; it is purely artistic, the mechanism of the brush, which we as artists always estimate. We do not look for it in Turner. Landseer is sensitive—delicate—with a fine hand for manipulation, up to all the *finesse* of the art; has brushes of all peculiarities for all difficulties; turns his picture into all manner of situation and light; looks at it from between his legs—and all with the strictly critical view of discovering hidden defects—falsities of drawing or imperfections. See to what perfection he carries his perception of surface—hair, silk, wool, rock, grass, foliage, distance, fog, mist, smoke—how he paints the glazed or watery eye! Turner could never paint any of these details. No! But can you tell what has become of the latest of his pictures, painted to illustrate a manuscript poem—'The Fallacies of Hope,' I think?

Don't you envy a man who has seen Turner paint these fine things, or who has shaken the right hand that did all those extraordinary works!

I have been blest with both these honours!
'Think of that, Master Brook!' Sir Edwin has
a fine hand, a most correct eye, a refined perception of character, and can do almost anything
but dance upon the slack wire. He is a fine billiard-player, plays at chess, sings when with his
intimate friends, and has considerable humour—
all of which Turner could not do. He looked
liked a farmer, and there was nothing about
him to denote the possession of great genius.
He was ruddy, and stiff in the joints; awkward
and ill-dressed, although he had mixed in the
best circles. He liked the retirement of his own
studio, into which he admitted no one, except
one or two particularly favoured friends.

I wish Mrs. Davison could have seen our meeting with my *old*, old friend, Tom Landseer, the
elder brother, who came to the hotel at King's
Cross to see us. We had been up to the Villa
during the day, and intended to start for home
the next morning. Landseer was not at home,
but Mrs. Landseer was overcome when we entered the house, after an absence of twenty
years. She hugged and kissed Mrs. Bewick,
and squeezed our hands, and showed us every-

thing the house contained, in her delight, and said Tom would be in such a way when he returned to find that we had been, and would be sure to come down to see us; and so they both did, and stopped with us till midnight. Well, my kind old friend seized my wife, and then me, the tears streaming down his cheeks with emotion. We talked so fast, and so much in the short time, that, being weak from recent illness, I became exhausted. We had all former times to talk over, and familiar and distinguished friends we so often met at Landseer's, so many of whom had passed from us. The scene became deeply interesting to all of us, and my sensitive friend was often moved to tears as he tried to persuade us to return once more among old friends. While I sit writing to you I am coughing very badly, for I caught a cold at the Kensington Museum. Long galleries, with open doors at the ends, and the sun burning upon the skylights.

My wife desires to unite with me in our love to you, Mrs. Davison, and Ada, and I am,

My dear sweet William, yours truly,

W. BEWICK.

Haughton House, near Darlington,
Nov. 16th, 1862.

My dear Davison,—I should like very much to see your collection of photographs from Raphael, and Michael Angelo, and Rembrandt. It is true I have not seen any of these fine things, except a very fine one from Raphael at my friend Landseer's, which is framed and glazed, and is hanging up in his studio by the side of a fine cast of the 'Apollo,' mounted upon something which raises it three or four feet from the floor. I had to look up at it, and it appeared very fine. The photograph is one of a Madonna and child, from a dark drawing in chalk, mighty fine! I was introduced at Landseer's to an American artist, who is in possession of an original picture by Raphael—5000 guineas— very fine indeed.

I have had an idea that Gibson's 'Venus' would disappoint me in regard to the tinting, but I was glad to be told by a person who has seen it that the colour is a warm flesh colour, for I was afraid it might be pinkish. I wrote to Gibson to mention what I had observed in some portions of the Elgin Marbles, where the wet or weather had not come, and it appeared to me that they had been painted with some kind of body-colour, perhaps with a vehicle of wax. Now, it is known that the Greek sculptors had painters to colour their statues, and there was one in particular who was famous for his success in imitating flesh. Some of the Greek marble is of a heavy grey colour, and this may have induced the sculptor to paint it, to improve the effect; but I suppose that all the varieties of tint would be given with the skill of a good painter.

At Rome, when rambling among the ruins, I picked up a fragment—a most exquisite foot of a youth—in this kind of marble. It was in the grounds of Cæsar's Golden Palace! I gave this beautiful piece of art to a kind friend of mine in London. I think I will enclose Gibson's last note to me. You will see what sort of man he is. He has the simplicity of a child. So had Thorwaldsen, who surpassed Canova, who seems to have been influenced by French taste, and whose general works I cannot say I like. Thorwaldsen's works are simple, natural, and very fine; and this reminds me of an ovation

I witnessed in Rome. Three German regiments passed through Rome from Naples, and the the commanders ordered all three bands to meet before Thorwaldsen's house to give him a serenade. Imagine three German bands united, playing their finest music, all the officers in the windows above, the streets crammed with the population of Rome, the simple, grand fellow, the sculptor, appearing amongst the officers, smiling with delight. This is, indeed, to be an artist! Can you and Mrs. Davison fancy this fine old fellow, with his massive white head, playing at children's games, such as 'musical magic,' 'hunt the ring,' &c. &c., among a squad of youths of both sexes, as I have really seen him do in the ancient city of Rome?

I am, yours truly,

W. BEWICK.

Haughton House, near Darlington,
July 19th, 1863.

MY DEAR WILLIAM,—When I awoke out of my sleep yesterday morning I could not help thinking to myself how exceedingly kind of you to come this way home and call at Haughton upon us, and give us the pleasure of your company, if even for so short a time as you proposed to yourself; albeit that my wife and I had determined to lock you up for the whole of the day, and send you off the next morning. But see how the finest plans of human thought are disappointed or frustrated! I had no sooner opened my eyes than Mrs. Bewick handed me your half-sheet of a note, blowing into nothing all our fine-spun plans, and leaving me and my two pictures, set for your examination and criticism, to silence and disappointment, till your highness be pleased to come and see us. The pine-apple pines upon its plate, the prize-strawberries sent from Richmond Gardens must be enjoyed by others, because, forsooth, 't' railway doesn't *fit*,' and the object of our expectation cannot come. So my wife, myself, my pine-apple, and my pictures, remain like fish out of water—as sad, as gloomy, as sorrowful as the picture of the three Marys that hangs by my side. We—the two who can—express our sorrow with 'open mouths;' and we express a conviction that no reparation can be made, or consolation imparted, but by your coming over and bringing with you the magnetic charm that attracted you so swiftly back to Hartlepool—meaning your 'better half,' *i. e.* Mrs. Davison, who, Mrs. Bewick says, must come for a few days for change of air, &c., and must feel that she may do as she likes in every way with us, and be at home as fully and as completely as in her own house.

You must have had a high treat at Tatton Park. It is true, when you see the finest things of the great masters, when you examine their dexterities of mind and hand, you are tempted to ask if there are no hands in our boasted school that can go so far as these old fellows.

I was lately at Raby Castle, and was surprised to find such a fine collection of works of art, paintings and sculpture. It is many years since I was in this famed old stronghold—famed in history and romance—and at that time there was literally nothing of art; but now there is a full collection, all of old masters, except one or two pictures—one by Turner, a good size, a view of Raby, with the pack of hounds in full cry in front of the castle. This picture reminds me of the painter to the King of Naples, who was paid by the square yard, and to suit his majesty, who liked a good deal for his money, painted huge skies—half his large pictures were skies.

Mrs. Bewick joins me in our best regards to you and Mrs. Davison; and I am, my dear Davison,

Yours, very truly,
WILLIAM BEWICK.

Haughton House, near Darlington,
Jan. 22nd, 1864.

MY DEAR DAVY,—I am quite aware of the results of body colour in water-colour drawing, as I used it extensively in my cartoons from M. Angelo, and I hope to see your success in it. I have seen drawings by Rembrandt when he had put white with his colours in the sky. Allan* showed me a picture in the Royal Academy exhibition, 'The Broken Fiddle,' entirely painted with body colour (water and

---

* Sir William Allan.

then varnished). It was placed on the right line, and was a beautiful picture. We are still proposing to give our evening, and hope for your company alone, if Mrs. Davison cannot accompany you. My bad cold has delayed our fixing the event, but we hope to be able to do so soon. Bonnington was *first-rate*. I admire his feeling and freshness, and breadth; he was very masterly. With our united kind regards to you and Mrs. Davison, I am, my dear Davison,

Yours ever truly,

W. BEWICK.

Haughton House, near Darlington,
April 18th, 1864.

MY DEAR DAVISON,—Now that you have sent back those fine drawings, and that your mind is at ease and your time more at liberty, I think I may venture to trouble you with a few lines, to ask how you and Mrs. Davison are after the fatigues of going through such a treat as Mr. Cromek has afforded you. Did you get to Byron Hall to the sale? I understand some things sold well, and others not so well. I am sorry that I was unable to go, as I hoped to have had a treat in the pictures, books and furniture, all which, I am told, were of first-rate quality. Bewick's birds sold for ten guineas; fine impressions are rare, or rather early impressions; my copy I bought from the hand of Thomas Bewick, and the impressions are fine.

Mrs. Cromek seems highly delighted with my introduction to the Misses Bewick. They have sent him a desirable autograph of their father, and they remember well the father of Mr. Cromek passing a night with their family at Newcastle. They also have sent him four letters from his father to Mr. Bewick, so you may be sure that the suffering invalid is pleased with those ladies.

What a lamentable thing it is for a man of such genius and power in the Art to be afflicted with racking pains and suffering, so that life seems a drag, and he is unable to realise the ambition for distinction to which his natural ability, hard study, and acquirements entitle him! His interior of St. Peter's is a marvellous piece of art and labour; how it is all made out and worked, and what delicacy and breadth is preserved! how flat the marble floor! The drawing of the interior of the cathedral at Sienna struck me as quite wonderful; so does the chapel at Warwick; but there are so many excellent things, that one is quite puzzled to select. With our united regards to you and Mrs. Davison, and to Ada if she is with you, I am, dear Davison,

Yours truly,
W. BEWICK.

Haughton House, near Darlington,
May 22nd, 1864.

MY DEAR DAVISON,—When the sun shines I am idle. Our friend Mr. Cromek is now in London, in the heat and turmoil, sweating in exhibitions or suffocated in omnibuses, fatigued by walking, and restored by Turkish baths! He seems disgusted with pre-Raphaelitism, and to get into the National Gallery out of the Royal Academy is quite a relief to his eyesight, and to his pictorial sympathies and tastes. He is a very amusing writer, and his tastes and judgment are refined and critical.

I hear that Cattermole and J. Lewis are now into oil. I think it a pity, if true; but Lewis painted in oil before he went abroad, so that he may be said to have returned to it again. I suppose they both wish to go into the Royal Academy, the members of which, it appears, will be increased to fifty. Mr. Herbert's fresco is making a great noise. I hear it is very fine, but in what way has not been explained to me. I suppose the scenic part of it is from photographs, and it is a real scene of the place where Moses is said to have received the tables of the law. The crowded host in the background, I am told, is very fine.

The season is very enjoyable. The perfume of the laburnums and lilacs coming into our bedroom, reminds me of sailing in the Mediterranean, opposite the Spanish coast, when I was walking the deck of the good Columbian Packet. The breeze brought a strange, bewildering aroma. I snuffed and snuffed, then asked the old carpenter if he smelt a delicious perfume. 'Oh, yes, sir; it is the smell of the vintage in Spain, which is wafted to us by this fine breeze.' Ah! what a time of enjoyment youth is, and what blessings there are in store for us if we only have the taste or perception to find them out, and the gratitude to acknowledge the gifts of Heaven! As I sit writing this short note, I am surrounded by such infinite variety of tint and colour and form of foliage, that I have abundant material for enjoyment in the wonders contained in the small space before my own house. You have the fine effects of the ever-varying sea, always interesting, always sublime. I am a great admirer of a noble tree, its arms and foliage, blown by the wind, giving to the scene variety of form, colour, and graceful movement; so also of a field of ripe corn moved by the breeze.

I am much obliged to you for the list of prices, &c., of the Spearman sale. The portrait of Bewick is very finely painted, and very like him.[*] Bewick was a hearty, fine creature. When I first visited him, after having been in London, he invited me to his house. The conversation about my aspirations, my enthu-

[*] Thomas Bewick, the celebrated wood-engraver, and now in the possession of the Rev. Edward Chase, M.A., Rector of Haughton-le-Skerne. By Ramsay.

siasm, &c., impressed him, as he had had feelings akin to mine when a youth; and he seized my hands, the tears filling his eyes, and encouraged me by squeezing them, and saying with the finest feelings, 'God bless you! I wish you all the success your industry and genius deserve.' Was not this very fine of the old hero?

Mrs. Bewick unites with me in our best regards to you and Mrs. Davison, and to Ada when you write.

Ever yours truly,
W. BEWICK.

Haughton House, near Darlington,
Oct. 23rd, 1864.

MY DEAR DAVISON,—It is now so long since I have received a scratch of your pen, that I have forgotten the end of your last conversation; so we must begin *de novo*, and try new subjects, if possible, to hit upon them. First of all, what is new to me is that my wife and self have been to Leeds for three weeks. We had pleasant lodgings on the side of a moor—

Woodhouse Moor—and we were quite in the country, although in the midst of Leeds. What a fine place for a breath of air!—always wind, sometimes storms. There the gay people of Leeds turn out at all times of day; and the women who have good ankles are rather glad to have crinolines to show their understandings.

We took a fine sunny day for Kirkstall Abbey, and were charmed with it. As a fine ruin, I think it is the most picturesque in composition of any I have ever seen. What beautiful pictures might be got of it! The east neighbourhood would be avoided, as the modern mills and manufactories jar with the sentiment of indolent monastic life that impresses you when absorbed in the admiration of the splendid architectural ruin before you. The intelligent old man that has charge of the place showed us two or three beginnings of drawings by artists who have to return to finish them. We missed the alder-tree that grew near the altar, from which 'Mary the Maid of the Inn' so fatally took a sprig, when the moon broke through a cloud, and she saw two men carrying a dead body. You know the story. The hat of one of them rolling to her feet, she took it up, and, carrying it home to the 'Star and Garter,' where she was waiting-maid, found in it, to her horror, the name of the man she was affianced to. Southey, in his famous ballad, makes her go mad. There is before you still the famed ruin and the said 'Star and Garter' on the same spot where poor Mary was fated to listen to the traveller's request to bring the sprig of alder at midnight. You fancy you see her — bright, beautiful, spirited, and firm of character — determined not to be daunted by so lonely and irksome an errand. The alder is gone, but we plucked a sprig of something else, to remind us of 'Mary the Maid of the Inn.' Curiously enough, the late Edward Pease, of Darlington, used to come every year to the 'Star and Garter' at Kirkstall to meet a Leeds gentleman, and these twain fixed there and then the price of wool for the season. The son of this wool-merchant told me himself this curious circumstance.

The ruin is in a valley. There are fine old trees growing in part of it. The river Aire, only a stone's-throw from it, ripples past the grassy banks, with boats and fishers, and every object to charm one who loves scenery. Then the river is backed on the north by wooded banks as far as the eye can reach.

We shall be glad to have a good account of you and Mrs. Davison; and Mrs. Bewick unites with me in our love to you, Mrs. D., and Ada. And I am, my dear Davison,

Yours truly,
W. BEWICK.

CHAPTER VIII.

CORRESPONDENCE WITH THOMAS H. CROMEK, ESQ.—HOMŒOPATHY—VORACIOUSNESS OF COLLECTORS OF AUTOGRAPHS—HAYDON'S COPY OF REYNOLDS' LECTURES—LIFE AND WORKS OF BLAKE—NOLLEKENS SMITH—ROMAN ARTISTS—SKETCH OF GEORGE THOMPSON—ANATOMICAL STUDIES—PORTRAIT OF T. BEWICK—TERCENTENARY OF SHAKESPEARE—MISS MITFORD—NATHAN ROBSON—PROFESSOR PEPPER—LORD BYRON'S LETTERS—FUSELI.

> Haughton House, near Darlington,
> Feb. 9th, 1864.

MY DEAR SIR,—I am extremely sorry to hear that you are an invalid. I sympathise the more with you as I have been myself an invalid for the last twenty years, and have been at death's door two or three times. I own with gratitude to have been greatly benefited by homœopathy: indeed I may say that I am now comparatively well, although still very delicate and easily fatigued; but I can and do enjoy everything connected with my beloved art.

We had Mr. Davison here on Friday evening. He brought a portfolio of drawings by himself and others, as well as a collection of photographs from the drawings by Raphael in the Louvre. My house is full of works of art, fine pictures, and a gallery, with a portfolio of original drawings by the old masters, Correggio, Rembrandt, &c. You may be sure that we enjoyed each other's society vastly. We had a large company of ladies and gentlemen, some possessing general taste for art, but none with the soul to feel it like our friend. He was delighted with some experiments of a chromatic character shown by Dr. Malcolm. This is one of Davison's hobbies.

I paint a little occasionally, and I am greatly obliged to you for the characteristic sketch of the poet Cunningham. You will see what Miss Bewick says of it, and of a larger drawing of the same gentleman. She sends for your acceptance the only autograph (of her father) she has; and I forward her note, that you may have her own autograph. It is Jane, the elder of the two daughters of Thomas Bewick: she has lately published her father's life. The younger sister is called Isabella. I have photographs of both of them. You speak of the voraciousness of collectors: it is true. I had no rest from them until I was denuded of almost every autograph I possessed of celebrated people with whom I have come in contact. I did manage to keep one, which happens to be framed and glazed, being a letter to myself from Sir Walter Scott: it is a long letter, and you will see that I could not part with it. I was twice at Abbotsford, and saw the great magician in his domestic circle. His conversation was delightful, very much in the Waverley style. The persons I met there were all distinguished for rank or genius. Besides this one autograph, I have others attached to drawings of celebrities whom I have met in society. The drawings are by myself in chalk, of the size of life, and are intellectually characteristic; and I made no attempt to idealise.

I am greatly obliged to you for your kind wish to send me your valuable book of original

drawings; and if you can risk them I should like very much to see them, if you can put in some of your own doing. Dr. Malcolm speaks of them so highly that I feel a great desire to see some. Your idea of writing 'your recollections' is a good one, and I have often thought of jotting down anecdotes and memorials of persons that have passed away and have become part of the history, if I may so say, of our times. Indeed I have done something of the kind, but it remains incomplete and sketchy. I am, my dear sir,
Yours very truly,
W. BEWICK.

Haughton House, near Darlington,
Feb. 12th, 1864.

MY DEAR SIR,—I am greatly obliged to you for the interesting book. The binding at once revived my Italian reminiscences, and Haydon's name too, with other associations of the past, filled me with melancholy interest. When I was in Edinburgh in 1824 a friend called upon me with a book that he said I ought to possess. It had been bought at the sale of Mr. Haydon's things, and brought to Edinburgh. This was 'Reynolds' Lectures,' in three volumes, with notes and sketches by the well-known hand. The work had been given to me by Haydon as a keepsake, and after I had had it some time he said to me, 'Bewick, I think you must give me back the Reynolds that I gave you.' So I took it back to him, and it was curious enough that I should be fated to get it by purchase after all, and in the round-about fashion I did. I still have the work, and treasure it as containing remarks and sketches by Haydon in his younger days.

He was an extraordinary man, a great enthusiast in art, and evinced wonderful power, as in his 'Solomon' and 'Christ's Entry into Jerusalem;' but after that period there was a falling off. He did not believe that man ought to be influenced by events, yet it is curious that his career was completely influenced and coloured by external circumstances; and if one believed in fatalism, one might say that he was driven by fate to the dire destiny which overcame him. And yet the circumstances of his early life appeared to promise the happiest results.

He married for love, his wife was beautiful, and yet his marriage seemed to be the cause of his ruin, for it was more than he could do to make 'both ends meet,' and petty worries and daily cares broke his strength of mind and crushed his genius.

I sincerely sympathise with you in your anxiety and vexation regarding the aspersions thrown out in the Life of Blake. Surely serious untruths, when published to the world, ought to be contradicted; the public ought to be set right if you are in a position to do so without much trouble to yourself. I have not seen the Life of Blake. Who was or is Nollekens Smith? There was Smith, of the Print-room in the British Museum—it is not he? Is Gilchrist a Scotchman? I think I have seen the Life of Blake severely criticised. But Blake, although poetically constituted, was sadly wanting in artistic acquirement, and his books to me are unsatisfactory. I have fallen upon a note from my late friend Captain Basil Hall, the son of Sir James Hall, who wrote his Travels to Chile, &c. If you have not an autograph of his, perhaps you might like to add one to your collection, and if I meet with anything else in this way I will take care to send it to you. Believe me, my dear Sir,

Yours very truly,
W. BEWICK.

T. H. Cromek, Esq.

P.S.—The copy of *Reynolds' Lectures* contains notes by my late friend W. Hazlitt, who had borrowed it to write his essay on Reynolds in *The Edinburgh Review.*

Haughton House, near Darlington,
Feb. 18th, 1864.

MY DEAR SIR,—I hasten to tell you that I have ascertained that Nollekens Smith is the person I supposed, late of the Print-room, British Museum. I remember him well. He was a notorious gossip, and I knew ladies who used to go to the Print-room to be amused by his endless and amusing tattle. He was a great retailer of anecdote and scandal, dealt largely in inuendo, and had a keen relish for any story of doubtful propriety. He had great expectations from Nollekens; and when the sculptor died looked to inherit considerable part of his wealth, but, like many others who live upon expectation, he was sadly disappointed. And he then wrote his *Life of Nollekens*.

I tell you what I know of the character of Smith, that you may not be annoyed at anything related by him. Nobody who knows him cares for or believes anything from Nollekens Smith. If you get his *Life of Nollekens* just for your amusement, you will, I dare say, see for yourself the character of the man. It shows the spite and venom of a disappointed man. I am, my dear Sir, Yours very truly,

WILLIAM BEWICK.

Extract from a Letter to T. H. Cromek, Esq. dated 29th Feb., 1864.

You know, of course, Gibson and Severn? Did you know poor Wyatt?—and then there were Uwins and Havell? Both the latter were sensitive and nervous. Havell never could be satisfied with his food! How he grumbled! I used to laugh at him. But I took pity upon him, he seemed so miserable, and invited him to dine privately with me at my lodgings. What a change came over him!—and as he praised the dishes set before him he seemed comparatively a happy man. He used to compare the Fratoria of Rome with his style of living in India.

Ever yours truly,
W. BEWICK.

Extract from letter to T. H. Cromek, Esq., dated March 7th, 1864.

The Roman artists were a curious ungenial set, take them altogether. There was a great division between the Scotch and English, I remember—but I seemed to stand very well with both. I took no part with either, but valued each man for himself, and always returned civilities or attentions. Gibson used to say, '*That* Eastlake, sir, is a curious kind of chap, you never know what to make of him.' He did seem to keep himself aloof, and was cold to many of the young fellows. But he was the first to take me to church, where he was one of the most regular attendants. He had been disciplined to this at a public school.

He was a hard student, and talked to me of 'the business of life.' Beginning life, too, with an independence, he has been a prudent and a most fortunate man, and now is happy with a handsome and talented wife. Everybody liked Wyatt, I have him before me with his guitar and his peculiar voice. It was very nice to see the two sculptors on opposite sides of the street so friendly, and Gibson sending visitors over to Wyatt's studio, speaking a good word of his talents and works. I am glad that Severn has become Consul at Rome, as he always liked to live there, and he will fulfil his duties well, and give great satisfaction, I know, to visitors. You will know he has lost his wife. I have not seen any of the young Severns. One of the daughters drew or painted small portraits very nicely.

. . . .

Ever yours truly,
W. Bewick.

> Haughton House, near Darlington,
> March 26th, 1864.

My dear Sir,—I have this day sent off the case with the smaller portfolio in it, and also my drawing of George Thompson, with the sketch done in Rome for a picture which has never been painted; for, as I said before, I lost the sketch for some years, and when it turned up it was offered to me, as a Wilkie, for a picture I then possessed. I have written what you desired upon both sketch and drawing. I am not able at this moment to state when George Thompson died; but I think it is stated in some of the recent publications connected with Burns.

As the Thompson is a chalk-drawing, you will be obliged to put it under glass to preserve it. There has been no copy taken from it. The spot on the forehead is quite correct.

I shall be most happy to give you an introduction to my intelligent friend Bonomi. How his brother, the architect, would be delighted with your fine drawings of the temples and buildings of Italy and Greece.

I send you the autograph of James Hogg,

the Ettrick Shepherd, friend of Sir W. Scott. It is the original MS. of one of his songs—he gave it to me when I visited him at his farm.

Ever yours truly,
W. BEWICK.

T. H. Cromek, Esq.

Extract from letter to T. H. Cromek, Esq., dated March 31st, 1864.

The picture in the Pantheon is the 'Lazarus' of Haydon. You are right about my sitting for the 'Lazarus,' which was all painted in one day, the painter being arrested three times during the painting of it. What a day! I sat for other heads. In the picture of 'Christ riding into Jerusalem,' now in the Academy of New York, I sat for several heads. One is very like what I was at the time; it is that of a person speaking loud to another, to give an idea of the noise and crowd. That other is John Keats, the young poet. Hazlitt, Wordsworth, and others, are introduced into the same part of the picture. Of course, they were all heads that suited the painter for character, and he painted them from life, giving the expression he wished.

> Ever yours truly,
> W. BEWICK.

> Haughton House, near Darlington,
> April 2nd, 1864.

MY DEAR SIR,

1 have a finished chalk-drawing of W. S. Landor done in Florence, with his autograph at bottom. Wilkie saw it in Rome, and said in his quaint way, 'Like! it it more than like — it is the man and his character.'

When in Rome I called upon a friend one morning (a Mr. Brown, a literary man, friend of Severn's), and a gentleman sitting at a desk, whom I had never seen before, joined our conversation about trees, their beauty, character, &c. I was very much astonished at the powerful language he used, and the knowledge he possessed of the subject. He went into the planting, the growth, the proper soil and situation of every kind of tree, and its particular capabilities and uses. His whole bearing struck me as being that of no common man, and afterwards I took care to inquire who he was, and Mr. Brown told me he was one of the most remarkable and talented man of the age, and was the author of *Imaginary Conversations of Great Men*, &c. Walter Savage Landor. I afterwards made my drawing of him, and he very good-naturedly gave me as many sittings as I required. He said, when speaking of tree-planting, that he had planted some large plantations upon an estate where he had built a mansion, and going abroad, had left his land in the tenancy of a fellow who destroyed all his trees and ploughed up the land. When he came back and saw the bare condition of his estate, where he expected his well-grown plantation, he was so disgusted that he pulled down the house, sent the tenant across the water (meaning he had transported him), quitted England, and went to Florence, and there I had an opportunity of meeting him.

The hands of Haydon are fine specimens of chalk-drawing, and are engraved by Thomas

Landseer in soft ground. It is to this Thomas to whom I propose to give you an introduction. He is a fine, good-hearted fellow, and, like his father, very deaf, but ought to have been a painter, as he is vigorous and spirited, and draws well. Many drawings of animals on wood are by his hand. I hope the next letter from you will give me a better account of you.

Ever yours truly,
W. BEWICK.

Haughton House, near Darlington,
April 16th, 1864.

MY DEAR SIR,—It is curious that you should have gone to anatomical studies first, like myself, who dissected at Sir Charles Bell's theatre of anatomy for three seasons with the Landseers. We dissected every part of the muscles of the body, and made drawings in red, black, and white chalk, the size of nature. These drawings were thought by the professor the finest ever made from dissection.

Your dear mother must have been a person of great energy of mind, and you have been fortunate in having her to encourage your advancement, and accompany you in your progress; and what a satisfaction it must have been to you to listen to her praises of your successful labours!

We surely take everything, or nearly so, of good or great from our mothers. We have just been reading *Family Troubles*, by Miss Hardcastle; and when I perused your account of your early life, it seemed so like a part of this book of cross purposes, that I laughed at the touches of nature you had described.

There has been a sale of book treasures, some drawings and paintings, and a portrait of Thomas Bewick, painted by Ramsay. I am sorry that I could not attend the sale. I have unfortunately got the skin rubbed off my left foot, so that I am obliged to wear a slipper just as if I had gout.

The portrait of T. Bewick that I possess was painted by Bell, in the style of Rembrandt, with the hat on, the light falling on one cheek and the side of the nose; and this, with the white neckcloth and frill, is the only light in the picture. It is artistical, but not a domestic picture by any means, and no one would like a family likeness to be so treated. But it is well painted, and I am often asked if it is a Rembrandt.

Mrs. Bewick will write ten thanks for the two photographs of the Misses Cromek. I have only to admire them. Mrs. Bewick unites with me in kind regards to you and the young ladies,

And I am, my dear Sir,

WILLIAM BEWICK.

Haughton House, near Darlington,
April 28th, 1864.

MY DEAR SIR,— So you have seen the memoir of me by Longstaff. I do not remember what there is in it. There are two other memoirs in two histories of the County Palatine of Durham. One of them has a line engraving from a painting exhibited in the Royal Academy. It was done on my return from Italy by a friend, now no more.* They are, perhaps, none of them exactly like. The drawing by Landseer was good, nearly life-size, but the engraving wants something. Mrs.

* Macarthur.

Bewick has found an impression from the painting, which she begs your acceptance of. It is well engraved, by (I think) Brown.

So your amiable daughters are amused by the particulars given in Longstaff. Well, my dear Sir, there is a great deal left out that would have been probably more amusing to young ladies in the way of romance; for, in the life of a young fellow like myself, there were often occasions for strange vicissitudes, both connected with art and other matters. The 'ups and downs of life'—all the vagaries of a chequered existence—hopes, ambitions, successes, and disappointments—hard work and anxieties—the 'fight' to get through the bogs and quicksands in the road of life—reality would be as romantic as a well-plotted romance, if we had only the skill to set it down.

We have been busy for the last few days with our tercentenary of Shakespeare. We gave a lecture with music, recitations, &c. The first lecturer in the North was invited by me to come, and being an old friend, he consented, and recited beautifully. He was our guest. He lectured here on Saturday and stayed over

Sunday. His name is Grant. He is a friend of Mulready, Tom Taylor, &c.; is a poet, and author of the historical romance of *Rufus, or the Red King.* He is also an artist, teacher of drawing, professor of elocution, and connected with the press.

I was present at a stylish Quaker wedding the other day. The chapel was crammed full, and outside in the street the crowds were kept back by policemen. Tell your daughters there were eight bridesmaids, all in the fullest fashion of the day; in white, with blue flowers or feathers to their bonnets.

The bride was elegantly dressed; she could not have been more so at Hanover Square. The ceremony was most solemn and serious. There was an address by an elder — (I sat with him on the same form at school) — dreary pauses — silence! The bridegroom, a handsome fellow, rose from his seat, took the bride by one hand, and said in a distinct voice that he 'took friend Maria Jane for his wife,' &c. &c. The same words were repeated by the young lady, the proper distinction of course being made; then a long pause of silence, and a tedious, gloomy prayer by another elder, followed again by a pause ; and finally the agreement on parchment was read aloud, and signed by the contracting parties, and any other friends. The affair lasted two hours.

The portrait of Thomas Bewick that I mentioned to you was for sale at a gentleman's house near Durham, and has been bought by the rector of this parish. It is a fine portrait, size of life, painted by James Ramsay for a friend of Mr. Bewick, of the name of Scruton, of Durham. Had I been able to go to the sale, the picture would no doubt have been mine. With our united best regards to you and your daughters, I am, my dear Sir,

Yours, very truly,
W. BEWICK.

P.S.—I have a vivid recollection of Miss Mitford and her father, but I have no drawing of her. Haydon made a beautiful drawing of her. She had fine eyes, a very happy face, and beautiful expression. I thought her very pretty, full of spirit and genius. She was fond of her father, who spoke with a Northumbrian accent, and had a boisterous, hearty laugh. He ran through two fortunes. After he had spent the first, he was walking in London with his daughter, and they stopped at the shop-window of an agent for the state lottery. She thought she should like to try her luck. It was on her birthday. So the father bought her a ticket, and she chose the number. The ticket turned out a prize of 10,000*l.* Could you think it possible that the father could or would run through all this? But so it was. He spent all she had, and was then dependent upon her genius and labours for bread and butter.

To see her genial goodness and affection for her father, after all the mishaps he had occasioned her, made one's heart ache, and kindled an almost enthusiastic admiration of her filial love and devotion.

I have no drawing of Turner. The last time I saw him was at the Royal Academy dinner. I was talking with Shee, and he came up smiling, and held out his right hand — the hand that has astonished all lovers of the brush! I have seen him paint (in oil). What a slobbery palette! what brushes!—what poverty of colours!

Haughton House, near Darlington,
May 5th, 1864.

MY DEAR SIR,—Your photograph has come home from the frame-maker, and is hung under one of Mr. Tom Landseer, and opposite one of Thackeray.

We are exceedingly glad that you are so much better, and sincerely hope you will be well enough to start for London on Monday; but don't hurry yourself. Should you not feel quite up to the mark on Monday morning, better wait a day or two longer at home than hurry away to strange lodgings. Do the Misses Cromek go with you? You will hardly be comfortable without them.

It is very curious that there should be two portraits of Thomas Bewick in the market at the same time. I should have liked to see the one you speak of. Miss Bewick will tell me if there was a portrait painted of her father by Raeburn. I never heard of his having done one. But I saw a very fine one by Nicholson at Edinburgh, and I have an impression that Lord Ravensworth bought it after Nicholson's death.

I wish you would describe the picture at Wakefield—size, dress, and if there is any inscription upon it at back or front, or date. A slight sketch in a letter will enable me to judge if it is intended for Bewick.

In the first Royal Academy Exhibition I saw there was a portrait of Bewick. It was No. 1 in the catalogue, and painted, I think, by Ramsay. He was dressed in a brown coat.

The Misses Bewick have a small, highly-finished picture by Good, of Bewick. It is a very interesting portrait, with his peculiar light and shade,—the lights crossing,—that is, a bright light on one side of the face, and another light, inferior, on the other side.

You quite surprise me with regard to the Water Colour Society. I should have thought members had priority of place.

I have had to-day a visit from the mother of the Quaker bride I mentioned in my last letter. She brought another lady from the south, a great admirer of art, &c. But it rained, and the fine horses in the carriage could not be kept in the rain long enough for them to see all I had to show them. They are both fine women, and dressed in the height of fashion. Quakerism is creeping out fast, both with men and women.

When I first drew from the Elgin Marbles at the British Museum, there came to me from Darlington a Quaker gentleman, without buttons to his coat—which was of the old cut and colour—hat of broad brim, and shoes with silver buckles. He was mild, smiling, and innocent-looking. His name was Nathan Robson; and I attended him over the establishment without my hat. I was then in appearance what you see in Landseer's drawing of me. The contrast between us was remarkable enough. This was the last appearance of the William Penn style of Quakers; and I have no doubt the Misses Cromek would have been amused to see youth and age so strangely represented. I only remember that people stared very much at us both. I had my port-crayon in my hand, having just left my drawing of the large group of the 'Fates,' or the full-sized drawing that I made for Goethe, the German poet.

The anticipated visit to Mr. Beresford Hope must be delightful to you, and I sincerely hope you will be able to enjoy the treat.—With our united kind regards, I am,

Ever yours truly,
W. BEWICK.

Haughton House, near Darlington,
Aug. 22nd, 1864.

MY DEAR SIR,—Both Mrs. Bewick and myself are extremely sorry to learn of your sad sufferings, and very much disappointed that medical skill does not relieve you.

Davison has been from home, but he has no cause of complaint against me, as I wrote to him last, although it is some time ago, and I wait in expectation of some kind of reply. At the same time, our intimacy is of such long standing, and we have so many tastes in common, that if I had anything to interest him I would not wait for his reply, but write immediately; and indeed I will now do so to remind him that

I am still alive. He is a nice fellow, and clever, and Mrs. Davison is also a great favourite with us.

We were invited to meet the celebrated Professor Pepper, of 'Ghost' notoriety, and of the Polytechnic Institution. I found him a very pleasant, joyous, and gentlemanly person, and his lady very handsome and ladylike. As I live in the midst of Quakers, he told us that he lectured at Stoke Newington to a Quaker's establishment of young ladies, and after the lecture they came to him with a set of difficult scientific questions, which he answered in the best way he could on the spur of the moment. After all was over the young ladies came forward, and each shook him by the hand, saying, No. 1, 'Fare-thee-well;' No. 2, 'Fare-thee-well;' No. 3, 'Fare-thee-well;' and so on through the whole of the establishment. I observed that the last young lady might have varied her good wishes by adding, 'And if for ever, fare-thee-well.'

My friend, with whom the Professor is staying, lives some eight miles from here, and the day being fine we enjoyed the drive very much, and arrived at home at 10 P.M. The dinner was a champagne one, and the grapes at dessert were excellent; I never tasted finer, and they were grown in the vinery behind the house. These was a kind of grape of a flesh-colour, which I do not remember to have tasted or seen before, and which was delicious. Our host is a sufferer like yourself, and was scarcely able to walk with me to see his garden, flowers, &c. We were boys together. He has a taste for art, and his dining-room is decorated with his own paintings—copies. He is now failing in health, but we had some pleasant recollections of early days. His accomplished daughter wrote to me that, as her papa was so unwell, she was sure a chat with me would do him good. He did rally, seemed in good spirits, and we had a merry day, with a good deal of laughter, in which the learned Professor joined most heartily, oblivious of his 'Ghost.'

And now, my dear Sir, I have written all sorts of nonsense with the view of amusing you, but fear that in your torments my gossip may be tiresome, if not annoying, to you. As soon as my photograph is ready I will forward it to you. From what I have seen of it, it looks ten years older than I really am, and *this* no one likes.

I wish I could get a cast of the bust by Gibson—profile—which is a fine work of art.

With our united kind regards to you and your dear daughter,

   I am, my dear Sir,
     Yours very truly,
      WILLIAM BEWICK.

    Haughton House, near Darlington,
      Sept. 20th, 1864.

MY DEAR SIR,—I hasten to return you the interesting photographs of your two old and valued friends. They are both intellectual, and both appear characteristic of truly English gentlemen, of the good old school. As you observe, I should not have recognised them, for time has changed both; but it has improved them, as their leading trait is goodness, which in young men is not generally so predominant as to be remarkable. I should like to see what manner of man Mr. Ralph has turned out, as he was a handsome boy, but a mischievous, harum-scarum fellow.

I do not remember to have met the author of *Hajji Baba*. As you are a water-colour hero, I will tell you of a singular character that was to be seen at Mrs. Chenie's—a young German water-colour artist. He was rather tall, thin, and worn, a shred of a man, as ugly as sin, with a voice like a trombone, and a noble genius. It was curious to see so precious a shrine in so rude and coarse a temple, and it was delightful to observe Mrs. Chenie—refined, elegant, and fresh—paying her gracious attentions to this uncut diamond. Her sweet and musical voice, and her delightful smile, irradiating her features, made her such a striking contrast to her guest that I have never forgotten either the lady or the extraordinary water-colour painter, or his works, but his name I really quite forget. Then there was an amiable Italian, with his guitar and sky-blue ribbon, and pimpled, crimson face. These were shining lights in the elegant crowd at Mrs. Chenie's delightful evenings in Rome. I think I met Mrs. Chenie at dinner at Lady Westmoreland's. There was my Lord Seymour and other gentlemen, and Eastlake—no ladies. I was unfortunate in being called to take the bottom of the table to carve roast beef, but everybody was too refined to partake of it. I have not half described the German water-colour painter. His works were landscapes, grand and noble in character.

Is it Mrs. E. Chenie that draws so beautifully? How enviable it is to be so gifted, and to possess so many resources of happiness!

With our united kind regards to you and your daughters, I am, my dear Sir,

Yours truly,

WILLIAM BEWICK.

Haughton House, near Darlington,
Nov. 5th, 1864.

MY DEAR SIR,—I hope by this time you will have returned and be quietly settled at home, and that you have had no renewal of your troubles. The weather has been for some time wet and cold and stormy, and I thought that you would hardly be able to leave Richmond, as you intended.

Speaking of Lord Byron and his daughter, Ada Lovelace, Dr. Malcolm showed me some of her letters, and said he had a few left. I thought of you, and begged him, if they contained nothing of a private nature, to spare one for you. Last night he brought me one of her notes to him, and as it mentions Miss Martineau's cow and mesmerism, it is interesting. I should have liked it better if her name had been in full, but we must be thankful for what we can get. Should you not possess her autograph, I trust you will prize her note as that of a lady of great intellectual gifts, and, as it appears, of singular spirit and independence of mind and grasp of thought. I have read some other letters of hers, in which her originality, I may say singularity of expression and humorous jollity, reminds one of her noble father and his extraordinary genius. Surely, my dear Sir, we live in a wonderful age. The age of Elizabeth was splendid for a galaxy of brilliant men of genius, and perhaps the present century may rank in after-times with any age for remarkable talent in certain lines, especially for inventive genius.

With our united best regards to you and your amiable daughters, I am, my dear Sir,

Yours truly,

WILLIAM BEWICK.

T. H. Cromek, Esq.

Haughton House, near Darlington,
Nov. 28th, 1864.

MY DEAR SIR,—I asked for the paragraph about young Stothard for you, and by consent I send it, to place with your other scraps about the family.

Mrs. Bewick is very much obliged to you for the copy of the beautiful lines on the death of Mr. Charles Stothard. It is melancholy to think of the sad end of the sons of so gifted a man as the father. Old Mr. Stothard was librarian when I was a student drawing at the Royal Academy, and well do I remember the first time I saw him in the library. He had a large volume before him, and he looked over his spectacles at me with a steadfast gaze for a long time. As I was bashful, this quite disconcerted me, and I blushed up to the ears; but his expression was so kind, and his smile so paternal, that I was soon reassured. I have often wondered, however, why he gazed so long, and what could be passing in his mind. I felt a great desire to speak to him, and to know something of him. I felt sure he would teach me something. I was then eager for knowledge, and anxious to improve. Nothing would have been lost upon me, if he had only given me a little encouragement. Perhaps he was equally modest, as I had no letter of introduction to him. I came more in contact with that strange but learned character, Fuseli, the 'keeper,' whose extraordinary language astonished and rather alarmed a raw country lad, as I was at that time—so sensitive that I blushed at my own name. Imagine my horror when a white-headed old gentleman spoke to me in language bordering upon obscenity, or swore like a trooper. It was curious in so little a man, with his odd figure and foreign accent. His peculiarities and his sayings were so odd, that more curious anecdotes were reported of him than of any other person of the time.

I am glad you continue to improve, and that you have finished your drawing of Rome to your satisfaction. I shall be glad to know what is your next subject. Mrs. Bewick unites with me in kind regards, and I am, my dear Sir,

Yours truly,
W. BEWICK.

T. H. Cromek, Esq.

Bowburn, near Ferry Hill, at J. G. Quelch, Esq.
March 25th, 1865.

MY DEAR SIR,—We arrived here yesterday, and I am glad to say Mrs. Bewick has borne the journey very well, though somewhat fatigued.

We had the better day for the journey, as there is now a storm of snow and wind that would have prevented our risking the chance of getting cold. As it is, I have a bad cold in my head, and last night I indulged in a good stout glass of hot brandy and water before going to bed.

It appears that Thomas Bewick, from great liability to cold in the head, kept his hat on whenever he could, and Miss Bewick tells me they made him a velvet cap, which he wore when at home. The portrait I have of him, painted by William Bell, has his hat on.

Whilst I was looking at a full-length photograph exhibited in a street at Newcastle, two workmen were looking at it at the same time. I asked one of them who it was intended for? They both looked at me contemptuously, not to know the great Newcastle Bewick; and one of them answered loudly, 'Bewick.' I said, 'Is it Thomas Bewick, the celebrated engraver?' The man called out, 'Aye,' in the Newcastle dialect. You should have seen how simple and innocent I looked, as if I had never heard the name of Bewick in my life before. I told the Misses Bewick this, and they enjoyed the joke vastly. Miss Bewick gave me Thomas Bewick's walking-stick; it is a blackthorn, full of knobs, with a silver hoop, upon which he engraved his name and the date; above that is a horn of some animal forming the gib. It is just as he used it the last time, with all the dirt upon the ferule, and Miss Bewick says he never had any other stick. In the full-length picture he has it in his right hand. Of course I bought the photograph.

I am sitting in a room at my sister's, with a large original Cuyp. In the picture cattle are in the bright glow of warm sun-light, whilst outside the house is a large stretch of landscape covered with snow, the air stormy, cold, and windy.

I should like to possess a photograph of your drawing of the library, even if it is not satisfactory to you. With our kind regards, I am, my dear Sir,

Yours very truly,
W. BEWICK.

Haughton House, near Darlington,
March 8th, 1866.

MY DEAR SIR,—In the midst of this fearful snow-storm one naturally asks every day, 'I wonder how Mr. Cromek is?' And I write to ask the question, trusting that he bears up wonderfully against it, and comforts himself by nursing a good coal fire, rubbing his hands together, and cheering himself and those young ladies of his who nurse him and are so fond of him. Formerly, in the time of Mortimer and Morland, they would have shut the window-shutters and got in some bosom friend, and with the gin-bottle and pipe turned day into night, and forgotten the storm in hot gin and water, or steeped their forgetfulness in the fumes of the weed, singing that good old moral song, 'Tobacco is an Indian weed,' &c.

But, my dear friend, neither you nor I can take to the gin-bottle for consolation. We hug our maladies, and try with the doctors to be resuscitated and made well again, and look upon this beautiful earth with the admiration that God has endowed us with the power to feel. You see what a stir has been made by the death of our old friend Gibson. Imagine, as you can, the man Gibson being aware of a file of soldiers firing into his grave, over the Emperor's graceful presentation lying on his coffin!

I will enclose some papers to the credit of the sculptor, which your young ladies can put into their scrap-books. They are written by one who knew Gibson personally, and is a great admirer of his genius and worth.

I have not heard lately of our friend Davison, but hope he is going on well; nor have I heard from Miss Bewick.

Poor Harvey! Have you seen what the *Illustrated News* says about him? The writer

appears to be totally ignorant of Harvey's
'Associates.' I could put him right, but do not
think it worth while. The writer, no doubt,
thought it better that his memory should be
embalmed in the society of *Sir* This and *Sir*
That, rather than speak the truth, and make
him associate with plain *Thomas,* or *Charles,* or
William, who were the real friends and companions of this clever and prolific man of genius.

Mrs. Bewick joins me in wishes, and hopes
that you are going on well, and that your
daughters are all quite well.

And I am, my dear Sir,
Yours truly,
WILLIAM BEWICK.

CHAPTER IX.

CLOSE OF BEWICK'S CAREER — HIS REPUTATION AS AN ARTIST — HIS TASTE FOR LITERATURE — POLITICAL VIEWS — ADVICE TO A YOUNG FRIEND — HIS ARTISTIC ACTIVITY IN THE NORTH OF ENGLAND — OCCUPATION OF HIS DECLINING YEARS — HIS DEATH.

WE now draw towards the close of a life which was full of vicissitudes. From the period when he left Darlington, almost a fugitive, Bewick had experienced many varieties of fortune, and had at last raised himself to a respectable position as an artist. The man who had acquired the friendship of Scott, Hazlitt, Wordsworth, and others of the more remarkable men of his day, as well as that of many members of his own profession belonging to different parties or coteries, must have possessed talents of a superior order — must have been endowed with virtues which recommended him as a friend.

After his return to the North, Bewick, as we have seen from the preceding correspondence, still continued to practise his profession. Although in his early youth he had expressed something like aversion to portrait-painting, he found it necessary, after his return to Darlington, to give way to the wishes of his numerous friends and patrons who were anxious to have their likeness taken by his hand. Darlington and the surrounding country includes a district inhabited by numerous wealthy Quakers, country gentlemen, and retired men of business, and there was scarcely one of these who did not desire to have his portrait taken by one who, they considered, had, by his career, done honour to the North of England. The consequence was that he was kept in constant employment; and the works of this nature by his ready pencil may be counted by the hundred. It must not be supposed, however, that he confined himself entirely to portrait-painting. As long as his health lasted he took pleasure in the production of historical and fancy pictures; and in the mansions of many gentlemen of the county of Durham, and the neighbouring counties, may be seen paintings which do honour to his taste and genius.

No artist can be expected to pass through life without experiencing to some extent the jealousy of rival artists or of carping critics. The claims of Mr. Bewick to any high rank as a painter have more than once been assailed; but without venturing to assert his right to one of the highest niches in the Temple of Fame, we are justified in asserting that the artist who received so many testimonies of approval, not only from the public, but also from brothers of the brush, must have possessed more than ordinary talent. It was no light gratification to an artist to receive the approbation of so thorough a judge of art as the poet Goethe, who, through the German Consul, commissioned Bewick to execute for him a large cartoon of some of the figures in the Elgin Marbles, that the German men of taste might obtain some idea of these sculptures. The poet was highly pleased with the work, and stated that his sovereign, to whom he had presented it, had ordered it to be placed in the Royal Academy of Arts, and would be pleased to know when the artist should visit his kingdom, that attention might be paid to him. In company with his friends the Landseers, he made full-sized copies from Raphael's Cartoons, which were publicly exhibited with great success. A head painted by Bewick at Darlington was mistaken, both by Wilkie and Calcott, for a Murillo. He also made copies of Rembrandt which few could distinguish from the original. 'The Kyloe Heifer,' which he painted for Mr. Hilton Middleton, of Archdeacon Newton ('High-priced Hilton'), was engraved by Turner, A.R.A. His picture of 'Jacob meeting Rachel,' which was exhibited in London and Darlington, was specially admired by many men of taste and genius, particularly by Haydon; and the figure of Rachel presented one of those evanescent expressions belonging to unripened innocence so difficult to portray, and which bore out Keats' opinion that 'Bewick would do some of the tenderest things in art.'

After continuing to exercise his profession for some time in the North, Bewick, who had amassed a sufficient fortune for his modest wants, determined to retire from its active pursuits. The interest which he ever afterwards took in art proceeded solely from the pure and lofty pleasure with which it inspired him. In his house at Haughton-le-Skerne, he had a gallery of paintings which was deemed worthy of a visit by all artists and amateurs whose footsteps led them in that direction. It was at all times a pleasure to him to exhibit his treasures; and his eye still flashed with true artistic fire when he descanted on their beauties of conception and execution. His correspondence, as we have seen in his letters to Messrs. Davison and Cromek, bore very much upon artistic subjects; and with the friends whom he collected round his fireside it was his delight equally to expatiate upon the subject which so completely occupied his mind, to recall his reminiscences of the past, and to amuse and delight all who listened to him by his anecdotes of his old friends Wilkie, Haydon, and Hazlitt.

Bewick also continued in his last, as in his earliest days, to cultivate the predilection for literature and literary men which had all along been so marked a feature in his character. He was naturally proud of the intimacy which he had enjoyed with Keats, Hazlitt, and Wordsworth, not to speak of the attentions which Sir Walter Scott and James Hogg had lavished upon him; and these reminiscences were not without their influence in giving a certain literary bent to his mind. The interest with which he remembered the distinguished literary men of an era that was fast passing away led him to hail the advent of new essayists, poets, and novelists. The works of Dickens and Thackeray afforded him great delight, and the comic spirit and poetic pictures of the one filled him with no less admiration than the deep knowledge of human life and the heart of man displayed by the other.

Though Bewick, on the whole, paid comparatively little attention to political matters, he was in his heart a true Conservative. The character of his mind—his love of ancient art—led him to be a *laudator temporis acti*. A friend of the artist's writes, 'During the years 1846-7, I had several opportunities of seeing and conversing with Mr. Bewick. I was then but a youth, in my "teens," somewhat ardent and enthusiastic, and having a firm belief in the "rights of man" as set forth in the People's Charter. Mr. Bewick was a Conservative, and in the kindliest manner combated my arguments in a way that produced a powerful impression on my mind. I had been attending meetings where the wildest schemes had been discussed, and plans for a revolutionary movement proposed, which fortunately were never attempted to be realised. Under these influences I became imbued with red-hot Republican ideas, and firmly believed that all monarchs ought to be sent about their business as speedily as possible. Mr. Bewick, however, from time to time, kindly reasoned with me, and explained how property had rights as well as people,— that if all were on an equality to-day, there would be a change to-morrow,—that reforms, to be lasting, must be, like the oak, of slow growth—and that the wild theories of the Chartists were utterly impracticable in the then state of society. Although my notions of "liberty, fraternity, and equality," were great favourites with me, the kind words and logical reasoning of Mr. Bewick tended greatly to lessen my enthusiasm for them.'

Such was Bewick's life and character, as represented chiefly in his own reminiscences. His latter years were almost entirely uneventful, no incident of importance interrupting the placid tenor of his way. Though he reached the period which is commonly considered the allotted span of man's life, he was generally free from suffering, and on the whole enjoyed good health; but it is probable that the remarkable assiduity he had displayed when a student of art, working from an early hour in the morning till late at night, may have entailed some consequences which would prove to him that the laws of Nature are never violated with impunity.

Mr. Bewick died at Haughton House, on the 8th of June, 1866, leaving a widow, but no issue. He was buried in a charming spot in the well-wooded ground which had been recently restored to the churchyard of Haughton; and the esteem in which he was held by those who knew him best was testified by the regret and sorrow of many who took part in that last ceremony.

THE END.

LONDON:
Printed by Strangeways & Walden, Castle St Leicester Sq.

www.ingramcontent.com/pod-product-compliance
Lightning Source LLC
Chambersburg PA
CBHW032132230426
43672CB00011B/2306